STUDY SKILLS

STUDY SKILLS

Establishing a Comprehensive Program at the College Level

By

JOSEPH E. TALLEY, Ph.D.

Psychologist, Counseling and Psychological Services
Clinical Faculty, Department of Psychiatry
Duke University
Durham, North Carolina

and

LAWRENCE H. HENNING, Ph.D.

Psychologist, Community Mental Health Activity
Munson Army Hospital
Fort Leavenworth, Kansas

With a Foreword by

Fred Newton, Ph.D

Director, Counseling Center
Kansas State University
Manhattan, Kansas

CHARLES C THOMAS • PUBLISHER
Springfield • Illinois • U.S.A.

Published and Distributed Throughout the World by

CHARLES C THOMAS • PUBLISHER

2600 South First Street

Springfield, Illinois, 62717, U.S.A.

© *1981 by* CHARLES C THOMAS • PUBLISHER

ISBN 0-398-04561-5

Library of Congress Catalog Card Number: 81-8888

Printed in the United States of America
CU-RX-1

Library of Congress Cataloging in Publication Data

Talley, Joseph E.
    Study skills.

    Bibliography: p.
    Includes index.
    1. Study, Method of--Handbooks, manuals, etc.
I. Henning, Lawrence H.   II. Title.
LB2395.T33   378'.1702812   81-8888
ISBN 0-398-04561-5   AACR2

FOREWORD

"**A** PROBLEM is simply the difference between what one has and what one wants" (DeBono, 1970, p. 279). A problem represents a difficulty, whether real or perceived, that interferes with one's progress toward a goal. In the case of most people the decision to go to college assumes a goal to be successful in college as measured by grades, the development of salable skills for future employment, or the personal satisfaction derived from having attained a significant body of knowledge. Evidence that this goal is not being reached may lead the student to the definition that he/she has a problem that needs to be overcome. A most obvious and direct source of remedy for this problem on most campuses is the study skills program offered variously as a class, a seminar, individual counseling, or advising. Whether these study skills programs are helpful in the process of problem solving may depend upon many variables including the actual nature of the problem, the potential of the student, and the effectiveness of the study skills intervention.

DeBono goes further to describe three types of problems: "the gap, the barrier, or nothing" (p. 279). Traditionally, study skills programs are based on the assumption that the problem for most students is a gap, a lack of information or skill that may be provided through an information or skill-building intervention. The student remediates this gap and thereby demonstrates success back in the classroom. A barrier, on the other hand, recognizes that the problem is more than a void and may actually be a result of a perception that has become so grounded that the person feels helpless to a point of impasse that thwarts goal attainment. Statements such as "I am too stupid, I am too lazy, studies don't interest me" are examples. To overcome this type of problem requires a restructuring and rearranging of the cognitive set, a reframing of the barrier in order to perceive options and alternatives that may make the goal more attainable. Of all problem types that most difficult to deal with may be

v

the perception of "no problem." It involves a lack of personal awareness that there is an alternative way of being. "This is the way life has always been," or "This is what my friends do — why am I not successful?" and typical statements of the unaware student. This type of problem creates a difficulty in finding a point of focus for one's effort. The lack of awareness becomes a major barrier in its own right. A therapy type intervention that proceeds through analysis of the historical formation of personal constructs may be necessary to develop insight into the presence of limiting dynamics.

Talley and Henning have presented in this manual of study skills a response to the dilemma that there are many facets to study skills problems. They consider the gaps of knowledge and skills by outlining behavioral approaches that use principles of learning to overcome deficiencies. They describe methods to more effectively overcome barriers and defenses. Cognitive restructuring examples demonstrate the way that defeating self-statements and limiting self-images can be relieved. They have even been so bold as to suggest the necessity of insight through psychodynamic approaches to alleviate those problems in which the student has little awareness of what is wrong and blocking progress. Obviously, the breadth of these suggested interventions from behavioral to psychodynamic will need to be delivered through various means. Methods for screening and placement into groups led by paraprofessionals or individual professional counseling is outlined. Inclusion of ways to assess the feasibility, appropriateness, and effectiveness of interventions are important considerations for anyone designing and implementing a study skills program.

The competition present in today's world has affected the college campus. Students are feeling acute stress to perform well and be successful in the classroom as a prerequisite for later competition to advanced educational levels and in the job market. The student, as consumer, is making demands of colleges to provide services for study enhancement. As educators, professionals in the delivery of these services, we dare not overlook the opportunity to provide the learner with a chance to reach his/her potential and to succeed in achieving academic goals. This book can provide a challenge and a stimulus for the building of study skills programs covering the full range of problem areas.

Fred B. Newton

Reference

DeBono, E.: *Lateral Thinking: Creativity Step by Step.* New York, Harper & Row 1970.

PREFACE

WHILE interns at the University of Virginia Counseling Center in 1977, the authors were tasked with the coordination of the Center's expanding paraprofessional program. At the same time there was a clear recognition within the Center of the need for a comprehensive study skills program for students; however, little staff time was available to offer such a program. We saw this as an ideal opportunity to utilize the eager and talented paraprofessionals.

Development of the program was more difficult than its conception. Many resources geared toward the individual student were found. Aside from some journal articles, however, no comprehensive outline existed to guide the student personnel worker's development and implementation of a study skills program. This book is an outgrowth of our experience. It attempts to fulfill the need for a detailed guide for the professional establishing a comprehensive study skills program.

Chapter 1 introduces our approach while Chapter 2 gives specific assistance in paraprofessional selection and training. Chapter 3 details the study skills program itself with a session-by-session outline. Chapter 4 is written specifically for the professional. Most students can be helped through the paraprofessional program. Nevertheless, some students' problems in studying are related to deep personal conflicts. Chapter 4 examines psychodynamic issues related to study problems so that the professional can assist in individual counseling those students whose problems aren't ameliorated by the straight forward procedures used in the study skills groups. A further elaboration of experimental and theoretical underpinnings is given in Chapter 5.

We thank the staff of the University of Virginia Counseling Center at the time we were interns, especially Barbara Schlepeutz, for encouraging and nurturing our involvement with the paraprofessional program. We are also grateful to the many talented paraprofessionals who participate in the project.

We would like to acknowledge our appreciation of the Counseling and Psychological Services of Duke University for sponsoring study skills groups. Alyce B. Williams of Duke is gratefully acknowledged for her secretarial support.

Our biggest thanks go to Kathy Henning for her editorial and secretarial assistance. Her contribution was essential to the completion of the book.

Joseph E. Talley
Lawrence H. Henning

CONTENTS

STUDY SKILLS

Chapter 1

INTRODUCTION

T HIS is a model of a study skills program utilizing a group format and paraprofessionals to assist in maintaining the program as well as in delivering the service. In this model the authors make use of relevant learning theory, including cognitive-behavioral as well as psychodynamic strategies of intervention. Discussion of the use of the psychodynamic and the more subtle cognitive approaches is difficult to find in literature dealing with study skills. Texts such as Deese and Deese's *How to Study* (1979) say in effect, "Here's what to do. Now, go and do it." This approach essentially ignores psychological or emotional difficulties that are often, if not usually, present and are integrally related to the study skills problem.

The presence of psychololgical or emotional difficulties is frequently a factor, particularly when a student has been at college for over a year or two and has still not developed or maintained good study skills. Generally, study skills are acquired by this time if there is no conflict in doing so; however, an academic price is often paid for developing these skills exclusively by trial and error.

In the study skills groups utilized in this model, skills are first presented and later followed by discussion of how these skills might be incorporated. This process should reveal the source of the student's problem. Perhaps it is caused by a skill deficit due to the lack of previous need for serious study, perhaps by a lack of practice, or perhaps there is a part of the student that wishes for some unknown reason to engage in self-defeating behavior. With this in mind, approach can be compared to Helen Singer Kaplan's *The New Sex Therapy* (1974). Kaplan's method also initially approaches the problem behaviorally and works with it at that point, then goes deeper into cognitive aspects if necessary, and finally approaches psychodynamic issues if warranted.

Recent needs assessments on college campuses (Kramer, Berger & Miller, 1974; Benedict, Apster & Morrison, 1977; and Carney & Barak, 1976) indicate that students perceive a need for study skills

3

services. In these times of accountability and financial cutback, providing the services requested and needed by the constituency served seems both ethical and wise. Many students at excellent universities are so bright that they have never needed to employ a systematic approach to study in secondary schools and are at a loss for coping with the sudden academic pressures of higher education.

THE GROUP FORMAT

Given that students of all different abilities and backgrounds appear to request study skills services, a major issue is the method in which these services should be delivered. To use professionals on a one-to-one basis is one option. If the bulk of the information to be imparted in these sessions is the same from client to client, it would be more efficient to present this information in a group format. The group would bring with it the additional benefit of students realizing that they are not alone with this problem. This realization is, in itself, very beneficial for almost any problem, as it relieves some of the anxiety about having the problem. Further, there often develops support and encouragement among the members and a sharing of ideas that may be very helpful in learning strategies for coping with academics such as overcoming obstacles specific to particular courses. It is important to acknowledge to group members that students may be more helpful to each other as regards specific information about certain courses and specific professors than professionals who often have little knowledge of these matters. Group members can also give feedback to each other about how realistic their strategies appear to be. This allows group members at some point to confront other members while the group leader may remain impartial.

The group format has been demonstrated to be as effective as individual treatment in many instances, including the treatment of achievement problems in college students (Bergin, 1971).

THE USE OF PARAPROFESSIONALS

Another aspect as regards mode of delivery is the possible use of paraprofessionals. The efficacy of paraprofessionals or peer counselors in working with their fellow college students has been well established. Peer counselors may, if anything, be more effective than professionals with college students according to a study by Zunker and Brown (1966). The use of paraprofessionals can obviously amount to great savings as regards professional time, and hence university dollars. This also allows the professionals a pleasurable change in activities (e.g. supervision and training) as well as other activities that additional time will permit. Further benefits include paraprofessionals acquiring some helping skills that will be relevant in almost any setting, along with some "hands-on" experience that may aid potential professional helpers in deciding whether to pursue professional training. Moreover, the paraprofessionals gain a sense of contributing to the student community and gather experience to cite on graduate school applications should they decide to apply. In a helping field these rewards should not be minimized. Financial remuneration is not the only form of payment; the rewards mentioned here may actually be of greater value than immediate financial payment. Considering the benefits to the paraprofessional, as well as the evidence that the student should receive at least as good, if not better, results working with a peer helper, it appears that everyone gains.

William F. Brown assembled a student counselor handbook in 1967 with the purpose of training student counselors to guide peers with study skills problems; however, this manual was written before the cognitive behavioral strategies described in this text were widely used and demonstrated to be effective.

The particular study skills program we describe here was initiated at the Counseling Center at the University of Virginia where both the paraprofessional training groups and the study skills groups were advertised in a brochure that announced groups that were offered by the center that semester. The brochure was circulated in visible places throughout the campus and mailed to likely referral sources. Initially, advertisements were placed in the student newspaper to gain visibility. The Counseling Center also served as a resource center for tutoring in various subjects, particularly mathematics and writing. Since the study skills program outlined here does not focus on specific subjects but rather on more general skills, it was helpful to have a list of tutors to whom students could be referred if help in a specific subject was needed. Joseph Talley also outlined material on and worked with the psychodynamic aspects of study skills at the Counseling and Psychological Services Center at Duke University.

In summary, the perceived need for study skills programs has been cited as has the effectiveness of paraprofessionals in dealing with study skills problems. It is also stressed that group treatment has proven to be as effective as individual treatment in working with academic problems.

Chapter 2

SELECTION AND TRAINING
OF PARAPROFESSIONALS

$\mathbf{A}$ PRIMARY task in organizing the study skills program is the development of procedures for selecting and training the paraprofessionals. Although the program is very structured, group leaders must demonstrate competency in basic helping and group communications skills. Assurance of this competency can only come through carefully designing effective selection and training procedures. This section gives guidelines for developing these procedures; however, the final result will depend on the needs at a particular institution and on the available resources.

SELECTION

An effective selection program depends on the identification of characteristics that can predict competency or gross incompetency so that unqualified students may be directed away from the program. This is best done by using techniques that are empirically reliable, valid, and efficient to measure these characteristics. Data-based support for such procedures is at present somewhat tentative. Nevertheless, some guidelines can be presented that have proved effective. It is important to note that the local institution must investigate the predictive validity of these methods for its particular setting and population.

There is considerable evidence that outcome in a helping relationship is heavily influenced by particular personal qualities of the helper, independent of any theoretical orientation or level of training (Bergin, 1971). This evidence tends to support the ideas of Carl Rogers (1951) that the qualities of empathy, genuineness, and unconditional positive regard are requisite for positive outcome. The association with these characteristics and positive outcome has been further supported by Truax and Mitchell (1971). Recently, however, questions have arisen about the necessity and the sufficien-

7

cy of these characteristics (Parloff, Waskow, & Wolfe, 1978). Nevertheless, these basic skills appear to be the basis of most paraprofessional training packages, and several methods have been developed to measure these qualities.

We advocate the measuring of these qualities for selection and training; it is the most reasonable approach given our present state of knowledge. As the situational variables that affect the relationship between personal qualities and outcome are more clearly defined, revisions in the procedures outlined here may need to be made.

Behavioral measures of empathy, genuineness, and positive regard lend a reliablity and predictive validity that is missed with the subjective evaluation made in traditional interviews. Furthermore, analogue situations can be used to provide a more direct assessment of skills. For example, candidates may be asked to act as the helper in a role play. The role play can be recorded, and the candidates subsequently can be rated on their performance.

Carkhuff (1969) has developed rating scales to assess basic helping skills that can be used to evaluate candidates. There is evidence (Anthony & Wain, 1970) that the predictive power of these ratings concerning basic helping skills increases considerably when the evaluation is done after a short training period.

Other personal characteristics of potential paraprofessionals are important to assess as well. Some evaluation of their motivation and commitment is necessary as training will take a considerable amount of time and energy. Persons trained who do not eventually become active paraprofessionals represent a loss in professional time spent in that training. Consequently, some predictive measures of who will follow through with the training and eventually serve as paraprofessionals would be extremely desirable. These instruments would most likely vary according to locale; however, some history of past commitments and the students' actual follow-through (or lack of) is perhaps the best measure. Succinctly, past performance is most likely the best informal predictor of future performance.

Most paraprofessionals who will be involved in leading study skills groups should be successful students themselves whose study habits are effective so that they may serve as models and can at times draw on personal experience. In selecting a group of paraprofessionals for training, it is also wise to have a demographic mix that is representative of the student body to be served. Experienced paraprofessionals may be used in selecting those to be trained as they have been through the experience and are in a position to ask questions from a different vantage point than the professional conducting the training. The use of the experienced paraprofessionals in selection is not only efficient in the use of resources but also increases the sense of involvement among the paraprofessionals themselves. All aspects of the selection process should be subjected to empirical analysis for the purpose of establishing predictive validity. Multivariate analysis of the different means of selection will yield the most economic methods. For example, if two methods are highly correlated, it may be unnecessary to continue both.

The selection team needs to train itself in the selection process, particularly when it has inexperienced members. Initial mock interviews can help the selection team develop a smooth and coordinated approach. Students outside of the selection team can role play candidates and give the team feedback on the interview. The selection team also needs to refine its rating competency, particularly when judging ambiguous dimensions in an interview. These dimensions should be made as specific and concretely behavioral as possible. Statistical analyses of inter-rater reliability informs raters whether they are each rating the same factor.

TRAINING

Paraprofessional training usually involves initial training in basic or core helping skills and then proceeds to skills specific to a particular position. In this case, the specialty skills involve training in the leading of study skills groups.

Core Skills

By the nature and definition of being paraprofessional, training is necessarily short-term and is less comprehensive than professional education. Ideally, the training program will include two to three hours per week during most of the academic semester. The focus at this first stage is on acquisition of listening skills, including reflection, clarification, and summarization of what a speaker is saying, while communicating a sense of empathy and care for the person being served. Also, some skill training in tactful clarification and confrontation to point out inconsistencies being stated by the speaker is relevant. The novice helper needs to learn to communicate caring without overidentification with the client. At this point much paraprofessional training tends to utilize behavioral techniques such as modeling, behavioral rehearsal, shaping, and feedback. There is considerable evidence that behavioral techniques in teaching basic skills are effective (Boyd, 1978). Although it is fairly certain that behavioral methods in teaching these skills are effective, it is less certain which elements of these different skills are most important. At this point supervisors' rational analysis guides the modification and synthesis of the training techniques to best fit the specific position for which the paraprofessional is being trained. Danish and Brock (1974) discuss four main programs that have been used in paraprofessional training that will be summarized here. They have reaffirmed that trainers must examine available resources and training models to determine what would work best for their particular needs. Thus, a wholesale acceptance of any one method over another is unwise.

The most popular training programs have certain common characteristics that may be used as guidelines for any paraprofessional training. The commonalities are as follows:

(1) using role playing as a practice technique
(2) recording the practice and listening to the replay for subsequent feedback
(3) all but one focuses on specific behaviors
(4) minimal theory is presented
(5) specific ongoing evaluation of learning is utilized

The following are brief descriptions of four methodologies commonly used in developing helping skills for paraprofessionals.

Microcounseling, developed by Ivey (1971), identifies specific helping skills and has a systematic training sequence for learning each skill. The skills include verbal and nonverbal attending, the reflection of content and feeling, and summarization. The training sequence for each skill follows these stages:

(1) The trainee attempts to perform the skill requested. Preferably, this is a videotaped performance that is available for subsequent comparisons to performance after training.
(2) If the skill is interpersonal, the client evaluates the helper

and gives feedback.

(3)   The trainee reads a description of the skill and watches videotaped models demonstrating good and bad performances of the specific skill. The trainee then discusses the reading as well as the videotapes with the supervisor.

(4)   The trainee and the supervisor now review the videotape made in step one in light of new knowledge and discuss differences.

(5)   A second performance is videotaped, followed by feedback and evaluation given to the trainee by fellow trainees and the supervisor. Further performances may follow if the skill needs refinement.

A second popular model for training paraprofessionals is that of *Human Relations Training* (HRT). This is outlined in the two volumes of *Helping in Human Relations* by Carkhuff (1969). This model focuses on developing the helper response dimensions of empathy, respect, concreteness, and genuineness. The helper-initiated dimensions of self-disclosure, concentration, and immediacy are also developed.

These dimensions are learned in two phases. In the first phase, the trainee learns to discriminate levels of the seven dimensions by listening to recordings of counselor models and then discusses the tapes and rates the skill level demonstrated by the model. In the second phase, the trainee learns to demonstrate the seven dimensions utilizing recorded role play and feedback. The trainee initially learns one skill at a time and then progresses to demonstrating several skills simultaneously. Finally, an integration of all the skills is reached, and the trainee has learned to distinguish the different levels of all the skills and is functioning at least at the minimally facilitative level on all dimensions.

A third program, developed by Danish and Hauer (1973), describes teaching the helping skills in six stages. During the first stage the trainees explore their needs to be helpers. This moves to the second stage, using effective nonverbal behavior, which in turn leads to using effective verbal behavior in the third stage. This is followed by the fourth stage, learning effective self-involving behaviors. Next comes the fifth stage of understanding the communication of others. The program ends in the sixth stage of establishing effective helping relationships. Each stage is learned through presentation, practice, and feedback. The program developers provide trainee workbooks and a leader's manual.

Interpersonal Process Recall (IPR), developed by Kagan (1972), is yet another training procedure. This process focuses on helping trainees understand the mutual impact in a helping relationship. This is accomplished by the videotaping a role-played interview and then going through several recall procedures. A supervisor or *inquirer*, reviewing the tape, assists the helper in recalling specific thoughts and feelings experienced. There is also a session in which clients review the taped sessions and are encouraged to recall their thoughts and feelings at various points. Finally, there may be mutual recall sessions with both the client and the helper working with the inquirer.

Group Leadership Training

After the core skills training has been accomplished, the trainees need to master certain group leadership tasks. These include some aspects of group dynamics and process, plus the specific content of the study skills material. In particular, the trainees need to learn how to attend to issues, such as subgrouping, handling detached members, members challenging the leader's position, and passive/aggressive behavior such as tardiness. The novice leaders need to learn to balance group maintenance and task orientation skills. They also need to vary directiveness, learning when to provide direct information and when to deflect member questions back to the group. Attention should be given as well as to the more difficult general problems of engaging members in discussion to prevent a strictly lecture format and, finally, to sensitive dealing with problem members who may be using the group to act out psychological difficulties.

Some overview of these difficulties as well as theoretical underpinnings, although brief, is necessary. Group leadership skills may be presented and learned in the same manner as the core helping skills. Specifically, role play, feedback, and videotapes are utilized.

Finally, the trainees must master the content to be taught in the small group setting. This content is presented in the following sections of this text. Supplemental material may be assembled from other texts or developed from personal experience.

As with selection, utilizing senior paraprofessionals in the training process not only is an efficient use of resources but also further increases their sense of involvement. Empirical evaluation of the training process, like the selection process, is necessary to ascertain whether the particular training package being used is resulting in the desired product.

The complete training program recommended is a two-semester package that involves two to three hours per week continuing over the majority of each academic semester. The first phase (approximately eight weeks) focuses on the basic helping skills utilizing methodology previously described relying on role playing and group feedback. The second section initially focuses on group dynamics and leadership and then on learning the actual material presented in the groups. In the next phase, the paraprofessionals observe one of the supervisors lead a small group through a two-way mirror, with an hour of feedback and didactic training following the study skills seminar. This highlights the modeling aspect of the training so that the trainees may see what the final product is like. Then one paraprofessional and the supervisor co-lead a group from start to finish, while the others observe through the two-way mirror, taking notes to share later in the feedback session. Finally, two paraprofessionals co-lead a group by themselves while the supervisor and other paraprofessionals observe through the mirror. Each of these study skills sessions is followed by approximately an hour of supervision. At this time, the skills are reviewed by the supervisor and other trainees.

By the end of this training sequence some paraprofessionals may be trained to run other structured groups such as social skills groups, while others will assist with training new paraprofessionals. This creates a self-maintaining system maximizing time input. Initially, a professional supervisor trains paraprofessionals. Then, they are able to assist with the training program. We feel the modeling aspect of the training is crucial. Even in professional training programs, a student may often go from start to finish never having seen an experienced professional helper work.

This concludes the overview on selection and training. Having presented the rationale and means by which this study skills program may exist, we now present specific content and a possible sequence of topics covered in sessions lasting from sixty to ninety minutes each. The length of sessions, number of sessions, and sequence of topics that yield best results should be determined by supervisors, paraprofessionals, and the students using the service. The sequence presented is one we have found most beneficial.

Chapter 3

THE STUDY SKILLS PROGRAM

PRE-GROUP SCREENING AND INTERVIEW

STUDENTS who come requesting to participate in the study skills group are scheduled for a thirty to forty-five minute interview with the leader. The interview is held to assess the student's problem and current level of functioning, as well as the appropriateness of the group as a treatment. The decision for participation is based on factors such as the student's reaction to the group format and whether the material in the program will cover target areas in which the student expresses difficulty. An assessment of how the student's personality will affect the group is also made. For example, if the student is withdrawn or manifests other personality and psychological problems that would appear to be an impediment to both the student's and the group's learning, other options may need to be considered. An assessment of how long the problem has existed needs to be made, because an underachiever of long standing is unlikely to benefit from the structured part of the group. Likewise, if the student is expressing general motivational problems and a disinterest in school altogether, personal counseling may be a better alternative. Moreover, the student's interests may be in the academic realm, but for some reason the person does not feel free to pursue other interests and leave this particular school.

An overview of the student's current life situation is important to assess stresses and conflicts impinging on the student. Asking what prompts the student to seek help at this particular time is important in evaluating the immediate problem. Questions about interpersonal relationships, especially a lack of close relationships, gives information that is often related to difficulty in academics.

Further, the pre-group interview should yield information about any specific academic deficits in mathematics, reading (vocabulary and speed), writing. These deficits are best remedied by tutoring, perhaps with the study skills group as an adjunct treatment.

15

Reviewing two or three returned and graded tests reveals error patterns and may show carelessness in test-taking, or perhaps comprehension problems. Frequently even at excellent universities, many students do not understand exactly what some words on a test mean, and remediation of vocabulary deficit is needed.

To some extent assessment continues throughout the group as specific concerns are addressed and re-addressed weekly. Nevertheless, it is necessary for the group leaders to understand the students' problems prior to the first meeting. This enables those best helped by a referral to a different mode of treatment to be identified and allows the leader to establish rapport with each member before meeting with the entire group.

SESSION I

As in the beginning of most groups, members introduce themselves with some personal information beyond names. They may just wish to state their year of study in school or major. Asking the members to discuss their hobbies and nonacademic interests creates a comfortable environment. The leader might then ask members to state their purposes for being in the program. Each student should give information as specific as possible about which aspects of studying are most problematic. The leader clarifies his or her role as one of sharing knowledge and techniques relevant to studying and of encouraging discussion and sharing between group members. This gives permission to students to take whatever they wish from the group and leave other ideas. Encouragement of group discussion relieves the leader from taking an overly authoritarian position. We describe the approach to study skills as experimental because students should try different strategies to find what works best for them. Since personality factors interact with methods of learning, very few, if any guidelines about learning hold true for all persons at all times. Each student must assess what strategies are most effective for him or her. We give a brief listing of the topics to be discussed and then move to the phase of goal affirmation.

It is important that in this session there be a reaffirmation of the goal and value of a college degree. This reaffirmation presupposes some basic clarification of career values so that students come to the group already committed to completing higher education. This commitment should be assessed in the pre-group screening interview. Each group member is asked individually to make a behavioral commitment to the group and to himself or herself by investing time and effort in accord with spoken values. A 35 percent increase in completion of reading assignments has been found using this type of oral behavioral contract (Birdwell, 1972).

Next each member is asked to set an overall grade point average (g.p.a.) goal for graduation and to keep this goal private. Voicing of the g.p.a. may foster a competitive atmosphere resulting in members outbidding each other with a g.p.a. goal. It is stressed that the goal must be realistic. That is, it must be consistent with abilities and with the time and effort the student is willing to invest. Each member is asked to think why that g.p.a. is needed and is questioned whether or not that need will provide sufficient motivation. This overall g.p.a. should be the average of a series of graduated semester increments in g.p.a. The first semester g.p.a. should be only somewhat higher than the present g.p.a. Again, realism in goal-setting must be emphasized. A realistic increase is generally one point (on a four-point scale) at most.

At this time, the notion of defensive goal setting as a protective device is introduced. Defensive goal setting can take the form of either setting a goal so low that failure is next to impossible or so high that success is unlikely but failure is safely hidden since the goal is recognized as being extremely difficult. Refusing to set a goal at all so that failure is comforted by the feeling that no real effort was made is another possible defensive posture. Fewer people set unrealistic goals after this type of self-deception has been considered.

This current semester's desired g.p.a. is now broken down into letter-grade goals for each course. Many students are here once again inclined to set straight *A*'s for their goals. We tell students heavily invested in this approach that of course they should try to do their best, but that the primary point is to avoid becoming extremely self-critical if all *A*'s are not achieved. It is sometimes difficult to keep from alienating perfectionistic students if realism is stressed to the point of acknowledging that all *A*'s will not be the best goal. We remind members that for most students to achieve all *A*'s the amount of study necessary may be so great that no free time exists; this absence of leisure time may of itself decrease the quality of study and leave students anxious, depressed, or emotionally exhausted. In this condition perfect grades may be unlikely.

Essentially, this is a *cost-benefit analysis* approach. We ask students to consider whether insisting on perfect grades is actually worth studying one hundred hours a week. We state that it might be better to study forty hours and be able to achieve two *A*'s and three *B*'s along with some fun and emotional health. The effort to achieve all *A*'s in the first semester might be likened to a long-distance runner insisting on opening with a four-minute mile in a twenty-six mile marathon. It seems that many students today would like to become study machines in order to achieve the goal of perfect grades. We try to help them make a rational choice about their study effort.

Task Analysis

Group members take class assignments in each course and break them down into daily or every-other-day assignments. Assignments should be defined in concrete terms (e.g. number of pages to be read, number of problems to be solved, number of pages to be written). Semester projects, including tests and exams, should be charted on a semester calendar. Times should be set aside for work on particular projects. The daily number of pages or problems may be put in the form of a chart to aid in monitoring study activity. The charting and monitoring of behavior as a self-help tool is described for use with other problem habits by Rose and Carroll (1974) and Mahoney and Thoreson (1974).

When possible a sample chart is drawn on a blackboard or posterpaper in the group (*See* Fig. 1). Each member is then asked to chart a specified period (e.g. three weeks) with days going across the top and number of pages to read or problems to solve going up the side. This may be done for each subject separately or for all subjects combined. Then the members take their weekly total number of pages to read or problems to solve and break it down into daily goals (e.g. seventy-five pages Monday, twenty-five pages Tuesday, fifty pages Wednesday, etc.). A dotted line is drawn connecting these daily goal dots at the beginning of each week. Then another dot is made each day for the number of pages actually read. When connected and then compared to the *goal line*, this provides a graph of progress and points out discrepancies between actual behavior and projected goals. The daily goal should increase gradually to allow for successful goal achievement by shaping.

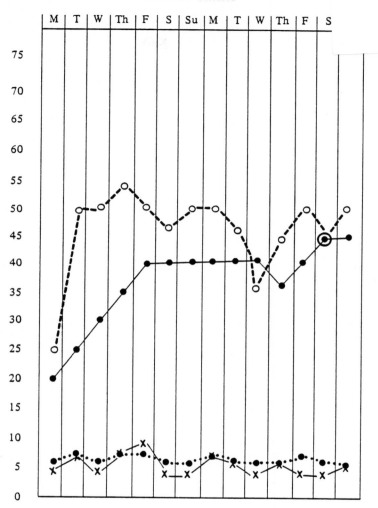

SAMPLE CHART

DAYS

Goal # pages read O‒‒‒‒‒‒O
Actual # pages read ●————●

problems to solve ●⋯●⋯●⋯●⋯●
problems solved X—X—X—X—X

(or, # pages written
or, # pages learned, etc.)

Reinforcement

Following task analysis we present the concept of self-reinforcement and its effect on human behavior. From a psychodynamic perspective, we add that the mind will not tolerate "all work and no play." Therefore, if reinforcing activities are not planned, the part of the mind engaged in study will be distracted with daydreams, etc. At this time members share some descriptions of the activities they find rewarding and fun to do. A few minutes spent in this way builds a sense of involvement and is an agreeable contrast to the more serious task-oriented discussion.

Given an understanding of the necessity and potency of reinforcement, the leader suggests that at the bottom of the goal chart should be a reinforcement menu from which to select upon the successful completion of a goal. The menu should include small hour-to-hour reinforcers (such as a phone call) and day-to-day reinforcers (like a movie), as well as weekly and monthly rewards (like a weekend trip).

Members should continually expand and stretch the reinforcement menu, listening to what others do for fun and utilizing fantasies of their own. Perhaps the menu will be made up of many enjoyable activites that have not been done because of lack of time or because the students have developed inertia from the "loser's syndrome." This is a pattern in which students feel guilty during recreation, thinking of all the work that needs to be done. Yet, concentration during academic work is disrupted by fantasies and wishes to have time for something else. As this circular pattern' continues students feel unmotivated, unhappy, out of control, helpless, and eventually, depressed and angry.

Charting, monitoring, and the reduction of large tasks into several smaller tasks begins to give the students a sense of control.

The discussion of goals, charting, and reinforcement should be a sufficient amount of material for the first session. Students are asked to experiment with the ideas presented, putting them into practice for the next week.

SESSION II

The first activity of the second session is a discussion of strategies attempted over the past week. It is best to avoid beginning the group with a discussion of scheduling as there often have been many unsuccessful and frustrating prior attempts at it. Presenting charting and task analysis usually leads to a more enthusiastic reception. However, the task of time analysis is done best with a schedule even if there is no effort to follow the schedule day by day. From time analysis the students can discover whether there are enough hours in the day to complete necessary work and still have time for some rewarding nonacademic activities. Results may indicate the need to drop a course or to withdraw from one extracurricular pursuit.

Time Analysis with a Schedule

Each member must design a schedule that will include the study time necessary to achieve the g.p.a. goal (see Figs. 2 and 3). The weekly time analysis schedule should include the subgoals of the number of pages to be read in each course per week and the amount of time studying per course per week beyond the initial readings. Consequently, each student must discover how many pages of a subject can be read per hour. Figures 2 and 3 are sample schedules. The importance of a realistic schedule is emphasized. Exaggerating the number of hours intended for study merely hastens the disregard of the schedule. This is, again, an example of defensive goal setting and might be pointed out as such.

Since many students still describe the use of a schedule as helpful, we also put forth the schedule as a technique to be used beyond mere time analysis. Nevertheless, the realistic approach described here differs from the scheduling approach most students have tried in the past. The number of study hours should be gradually increased so that the student may be successful in keeping the schedule while improving study behavior. Here again is the possibility of another pitfall; students may schedule an increase in study hours too abruptly, thus denying the need to gradually adjust to a change in life-style. If the schedule is excessively demanding, frustration may lead to abandoning it. In keeping with cognitive dissonance theory, either the schedule or the enjoyable activities will have to be sacrificed, and most likely it will be the schedule.

This schedule is to be revised periodically, and problems in constructing it are discussed in group meetings in which members can

FIGURE 2. SAMPLE SCHEDULE

	Monday	Tuesday	Wednesday
7 AM	breakfast, shower, dress, go to campus		
8 AM	history	read 20 pp.	history
	class	English	class
9 AM	calculus	English	calculus
	class	class	class
10 AM	15 min. break		15 min. break
	review &	15 min. break	review &
	reorganize	pleasure	reorganize
	notes	activity	notes
11 AM	chemistry		chemistry
	lecture		lecture
12 noon	lunch		
1 PM	chemistry	sociology	read 30 pp.
	lab	class	English
2 PM		break	
3 PM		5 calculus	catch up
		problems	or reorganize
4 PM	break	notes	
5 PM		read 20 pp.	leisure
		sociology	
6 PM	supper		
7 PM	read 20 pp.	read 20 pp.	5 chemistry
	calculus	chemistry	problems
8 PM	break	break	break
9 PM	read 30 pp.	read 30 pp.	socialize or
10 PM	calculus	chemistry	activity
11 PM	sleep		

Task Analysis for Week

sociology	read	100 pages
English	read	100 pages
chemistry	read	50 pages
	work	10 problems
calculus	read	50 pages
	work	10 problems
history	read	100 pages

FIGURE 2. (continued)

Thursday	Friday	Saturday	Sunday
read 20 pp. English English class	history class calculus class	sleep late	
15 min. break pleasure activity	15 min. break review & reorganize notes chemistry lecture	read 40 pp. history	
sociology class break 5 calculus problems break read 20 pp. sociology	semester long projects break semester long projects	outside activity or a trip	read 40 pp. history
5 chemistry problems break read 30 pp. English		party	read 20 pp. history

List of Reinforcement Rewards

Daily: listen to album
           make phone call
           socialize
           coffee, coke
Weekly: movie
           shopping
           party
           trip
           social activity

Even with a very heavy academic schedule there is time for eight hours sleep per night, three meals, most of the weekend off, most of one evening during the week off, frequent breaks and leisure. Note getting the body rhythm trained by eating meals and taking breaks at same time each day if possible.

Study Skills

FIGURE 3. SAMPLE SCHEDULE

	Monday	Tuesday	Wednesday
7 AM	breakfast, shower, dress, go to class		
8 AM	accounting class	biology lab	accounting class
9 AM	biology lecture		biology lecture
10 AM	read 20 pp.		French lab
11 AM	accounting		
12 noon	lunch		
1 PM	read 30 pp. management	read 20 pp. accounting	economics class
2 PM			break
3 PM	break	break read 25 pp.	French class
4 PM	read 25 pp. biology	biology	
5 PM			break 5 economics problems
6 PM	supper		
7 PM	management class	student government fraternity meeting	break
8 PM			
9 PM	committee		
10 PM	break		meeting
11 PM	sleep		

Task Analysis for Week

biology	read	50 pages
accounting	read	40 pages
	work	10 problems
economics	read	40 pages
	work	10 problems
management	read	60 pages
French	read and study	
	40 pages	

FIGURE 3. (continued)

Thursday	Friday	Saturday	Sunday
read 20 pp. accounting	accounting class	job	sleep late
break	biology		
read & study	lecture		
20 pp. French	read & study		
	20 pp. French		church
read 30 pp. management	economics class	job	read 20 pp. economics
			break
read 20 pp.	French		semester
read 20 pp.	class		projects
break	break		
5 accounting problems	5 economics problems		
read & study	party	party	semester
20 pp. French			projects
break			& catch up

Reinforcement Menu

This student appears to be overextended. There is little time uncommited. A sudden unexpected assignment such as an extra paper to write would be very difficult.

daily weekly	1.	
	2.	
	3.	
	4.	
	5.	
	6.	
	7.	
monthly	8.	
	9.	
semester	10.	
	11.	
year	12.	

give feedback on how realistic the schedule appears to be. In making up the schedule, individual differences must be taken into account. These can be discovered only through experimentation. Some persons study more effectively in the morning while others study more effectively in the evening. Further, individual differences will arise about what course should be studied when. For example, for some people English may be studied more easily in the evening than calculus. Some academic work may be done better during brief periods (e.g. between classes), while other work such as chemistry may require a longer period of time for concentration. In constructing the schedule, study periods of sixty to ninety minutes by breaks of ten to fifteen minutes are put forth as the usual optimum. The breaks consist of the use of reinforcements that are part of the reinforcement menu, such as listening to an album or making a phone call. Some of the reinforcements will be for a ninety-minute period of study, some for an evening of study, and others for a successful week of study or a successful semester of study. These are similar to rewards used in the charting and monitoring techniques. Consequently, some of the reinforcements will only last a few minutes while others may last an entire weekend or week. The actual scheduling of these reinforcements makes the schedule both realistic and rewarding.

Students taking fifteen hours a week in class may spend maximally thirty to forty-five hours outside of class studying. Therefore, the entire responsibility of school may take from forty-five to sixty hours a week if there are no problems with study techniques and concentration. Students' lives may be compared to those of people having full-time jobs requiring ten hours a day, six days a week, with considerable time still remaining for other activities. Often when this is calculated in front of students, showing in this case most of every evening and one full day per week free, students appear to be in a state of disbelief. To students the work load feels endless. This is often due to ruminating and obsessing about what should be done to the point that the student cannot enjoy any recreation. Consequently, part of the student that has felt no pleasure rebels and insists upon some daydreaming throughout the studying. Of course, the daydreaming reduces the quality and amount of work done, and the student feels guilty because so little has been accomplished. All of this culminates in increased obsessing and ruminating to the point that debilitating anxiety abounds, and the student follows the downward spiral of passive resignation, sluggishness, and uninvolvement.

Others may systematically avoid academic work by requiring that everything in a room be just right before they can begin, or by insisting that all laundry be done, clothes ironed, etc. Some healthy compartmentalization in students' lives is gained by using a schedule. Recreation is no longer disturbed by guilt and fear that there will be no time for work. Work that is broken down into daily portions appears more manageable. A sense of control is restored.

Elaborating on the syndromes and patterns described gives students a sense that the leader does understand their study problems.

Place of Study

Next the topic of where to study is introduced. Members are asked to describe where they study and what, if anything, is helpful about that place. We suggest that the study place be viewed as a discriminative stimulus for studying just as a light may be the discriminative stimulus for a pigeon to peck for a reward. The concept of discriminative stimuli is explained to the group. They are told that a certain environment X (sitting at a desk) may be the discriminative stimulus for Y (studying). Ideally, no other activity, especially recreational, is done at the desk. Therefore, if students find themselves sleeping at the usual place of work, they must move in order to keep the place of study a discriminative stimulus or cue for the response of studying. We stress that much of the effect of cues on response patterns occurs outside of awareness. We would not pretend that the same type of study environment is best for all. It appears that many students do better work with soft music in the background despite all the typical recommendations that study be done in silence. Many treatments, such as the use of stimulants to calm hyperactive children, do not make apparent sense, yet they work. This is part of why we encourage experimental, individual differences, or ideographic approach to study skills.

SESSION III

Again, the session opens with the sharing of charts and schedules as well as the variations that have been incorporated. This process encourages both continued use of time management tools as well as continued analysis of behavioral patterns. At this point resistance to using charts or schedules may be heard and discussed. During this discussion it is important to keep the group leader from appearing to be a parental figure interested in enforcing demands; reflecting questions back to group members may accomplish this as well as being very helpful to the students. Another strategy that is helpful at this point in avoiding an impasse is framing the problem in terms of parts of the self. This approach clarifies and amplifies that a part of the student wishes to study while another part wishes to avoid studying and obtains some benefits for doing so. Some strategies involving the exploration of "self talk" or internal narrations (Meichenbaum & Cameron, 1974) powerfully underscore the reality that these two parts and sets of thoughts coexist. For instance, members may be asked what thoughts go through their minds as they begin or are in the midst of study. With sufficient probing, the self-statements and beliefs that lead to maladaptive studying should become clear. This is one of the most important aspects of the entire study skills seminar, that is, helping students to see that a part of them does wish to study very diligently while another part of them is often resistant to study. This message is given while communicating that this conflict is not at all an unusual problem.

Schedules and charts are circulated among the group members, followed by mutual questioning about whether their schedules appear realistic. Hopefully, this promotes a belief that scheduling and charting may be valuable tools for change. Many clients sabotage their self-management by not believing in the usefulness of these tools. They might say, for instance, "I've tried scheduling before, and it doesn't work." The group leader, along with fellow members, must be prepared to clarify that it was not the schedule itself that failed to produce results but rather that the client chose to abandon it. This defensive process is usually begun by constructing an unrealistic schedule with no subsequent modifications, as a schedule that may cause resentment because of the loss of freedom it imposes. Without sounding punitive, the message should be given that now a more satisfying schedule may be composed in light of ideas presented in the group. The leader or group members might humorously note that this new schedule has been neither written up by the university nor mailed from home, but that it represents a free choice by a student to restrain some present freedom in exchange for other enjoyable things in the future.

This, of course, may open a Pandora's box of possible disillusionment and questioning, given the possibility that study efforts, even if successful, may be in vain considering the current employment market. Our response is to honestly acknowledge that there may be no financial advantage with the bachelor's degree and a good grade point average. Spending time and effort may not pay off financially and thus may be a gamble, but forgetting about good grades while getting a degree is also a gamble. We ask students to review some of the reasons they have committed themselves to completion of college. It is emphasized that a fatalistic attitude can be nothing but debilitating. Likewise, concentrating on the possible lack of rewards for effort is encouraging a half-hearted effort.

Other more specific scheduling difficulties arise with members; for example, some find it difficult to resist friendly visitors. These difficulties must be approached from a case by case method and often some assertiveness training along the lines of that outlined by Jakubowski and Lange (1976) is incorporated to help the student feel more comfortable in social disengagement. Difficulty in socially disengaging during a planned study time appears to be one of the most important problems in poor study habits. Role plays of disengaging behavior may be incorporated in the format at this time.

As with assertiveness training, it is important to explore underlying assumptions and cognitions that make it difficult for the person to disengage. For some, the excessive need for affiliating appears to be motivated by their own dependency needs; for others, there appears to be a fear of hurting friends' feelings; still others feel that being assertive in general is wrong. We initially discuss surface cognitions and then help members discover their underlying beliefs. For example, a surface level thought when considering social disengaging may be, "If I leave I will hurt my friends' feelings." Beneath this might be the belief, "If I don't always go with my friends when they want me to go and if I hurt their feelings by rejecting them, they will stop being my friends." This in turn rests on an underlying assumption that may be something like, "People won't like me if I do not do as they wish me to do," or stated more generally, "One should not be assertive or do things solely for the benefit of him or herself."

Meichenbaum and Cameron (1974) have dealt with how our self-talk (the subjective covert narration of events going on in our heads) influences what we do. Meichenbaum and his associates have used *positive self-talk* or *coping statements* to counter negative or debilitating self-statements with schizophrenics, impulsive children, neurotics, and test-anxious college students. The paradigm is also suitable for use with study skills. Group members all offer examples of typical self-defeating statements such as the following:

> This is boring.
> I'll never learn this.
> Maybe I'll go visit someone.
> What good will it do me to learn this?
> I'll cram later on.
> It's all a matter of luck anyway.
> This isn't relevant to me and my life.

Each student may then arrange counterstatements for whatever specific self-defeating thoughts he or she may have; group members also offer counterstatements to each other for use in defeating this negativistic thinking. The use of counterstatements may be practiced in the group. One procedure is to do a role play in which the leader plays the negative voice. This can be a psychodrama between conflicting parts of the student, and the student can provide counterstatements. This usually results in a role play with a high degree of emotional involvement.

For example, "This is boring," may be countered with a statement such as, "It may be boring, but it is also leading to something that is important, something I don't want to lose!" Certain self-coaching is rehearsed to be used covertly. For example, the thought, "I'll never learn this," may be countered with, "Unless I believe I can learn this, then I certainly will not. Think about how good it will feel to show that I know this on the test."

Other counterarguments to be incorporated may run along the lines of "If I wasn't able to learn this I wouldn't be here," or "I can't be positive that I will use this, but it is probable that at some time I will need this knowledge to build upon even though I am not aware of this now." Such thoughts as "What good will it do me to learn this?" are countered by "It's too early in the game to narrow my goals; I may need this knowledge sometime after all." "I'll cram later on," may be countered with some self-confrontation: "Let's quit kidding; I said that last time." "It's all a matter of luck," can be countered with "Maybe some luck is involved, but those who study best usually make the better grades," and self-talk such as "I want to grow a little, to expand my life and interests so that more things will be relevant."

The actual acting out of these statements is encouraged along with other self-enhancing coping statements of a general nature such as the following:

Doing fine!
What's this?
I'll have to try this section again!
Good now!
I've got it!

What this essentially amounts to is cognitive rehearsal. As with behavioral rehearsal, the cognitions may first be modeled aloud by the group leader, then used by the group members in their psychodrama, and finally incorporated and rehearsed covertly by the group members. Follow-up on whether the student finds this helpful is suggested. At this point, it should be noted that the counterstatements must be accepted as legitimate and potent by students and not simply suggested or imposed by the group leader. With the role plays as well as members exchanging feedback, ample material has been covered for the session.

SESSION IV

Once more the session is opened with questions about which techniques group members have been trying, what has been working, and what has been difficult to implement. Students may refer back to charts, schedules, and modifications of these or may focus on more recent topics such as the self-statements and the ability to socially disengage. Thoughts that tend to disrupt study might be examined again. If any member of the group seems to have a consistent theme in his or her distracting thoughts, individual counseling may be recommend.

The review of disrupting thoughts leads logically to the next topic of concentration. Lack of concentration is generally due to some undesirable self-talk or to thoughts that seem to occur automatically and are difficult to dismiss. These internal dialogues may severely limit concentration. Nevertheless, some behavioral techniques may be used to support the cognitive interventions. Some techniques we have found effective are as follow:

(1) The student can take the responsibility to close the book as soon as daydreaming begins. This is a self-confrontation that studying is not taking place. Something about an open book assuages guilt.

(2) A piece of scrap paper can be kept to the side of the book as a place to write down one- or two-word cues for seducing, unrelated thoughts that promise to be too precious or crucial to cast away while studying. Students can plan to go back after studying and consider these thoughts which seemed to be so weighty. It is often surprising how these thoughts no longer appear to be so crucial at that time.

(3) A technique used less often is that of wearing a rubber band around the wrist that can be "popped" when daydreaming takes place.

(4) Finally, students can be asked to gather baseline data by keeping records of how many times daydreaming occurs during an hour. This can be very confronting and can of itself lead to behavior change. This, too, can be done by keeping a piece of paper at the side of the book and simply making a check each time daydreaming occurs.

Perhaps the most important aspect of inner conflict as regards motivation and concentration is the necessity of asking the basic question, "Do I wish to do this or not? I am in charge of my life, and if I do not wish to do this I may leave; however, if I am going to attempt this endeavor, I'd better get down to business." This simply means reminding oneself that he or she is choosing to do this. If for some students this is not the case, then the materials concerning the psychodynamic issues with study skills problems may be the most relevant.

SESSION V

This session is best begun by asking members for their reactions to the content of Session IV as well as whether any behavioral interventions were utilized during the week. If no such interventions were employed, it is helpful to explore what got in the way of trying the techniques. Devoting quite a bit of time to this should prove profitable. It is the core of motivation and leads to the deeper psychodynamic factors that may greatly influence outcome.

SQ3R

The so-called SQ3R method of study is described in most current texts on study skills. SQ3R is an abbreviation for *s*urvey, *q*uestion, *r*ead, *r*ecall, *r*eview. This title may sound somewhat technical in the abbreviated form, but it simply stands for the old preacher's method: "First I tell 'em what I'm gonna tell 'em; then I tell 'em; and then I tell 'em what I told 'em." This model is still followed in television newscasts. We first hear what is soon to be reported (survey), then we hear the actual content (read), and finally we are told in a recap what we have heard (review).

The first stage of SQ3R is *surveying* the material. This consists of looking over the preface, the table of contents, and the introduction to get an idea of what the book will cover. Surveying should also be done in a more specific manner before reading each chapter. The title of the chapter, its introduction, subheading, and conclusion or summary are surveyed to inform the reader of the information to be given and the types of questions to be answered. The reader gets an overview of how this chapter relates to the preceding chapter and the following one, as well as how it fits into the framework of the entire book. Surveying what is to be read gives an "advance organizer" or structure in which to place the material. This is analogous to the skeleton's function in anatomy. Further, surveying begins the process of grouping and clustering content, resulting in improved comprehension and recall of material.

Next, the *question* stage consists of posing to oneself the questions this body of information is supposed to answer. One method of doing this is to reword chapter subheadings and other headings to form questions. In gestalt terminology, the questions then create an open figure that needs closure with the answers that follow when reading. The ability to pose good questions is a skill that takes time to develop. By reviewing questions on examinations, the student may eventually learn to ask study questions similar to those that the course instructor would design. Questions typically asked might include the following:

What is X?
How does it work?
What evidence supports this?
What is the evidence to the contrary?

The library is full of books with queries such as these written in the margins, and we may have wondered what type of person would do this. However destructive of property this person may have been, we feel convinced that this reader understood the material and walked away with a *working* comprehension versus simply knowing what the material was about. In some ways, this approach makes the interaction with the book similar to an interpersonal interaction, with an exchange of questions and follow-ups that is often easier to remember than straight information from reading.

During the *reading* phase, next, there is an emphasis on continued questioning of the material. Questions such as "How does this work?" "What else was happening in that time in history?" and "How does this pertain to yesterday's reading?" are presented as examples. Reading involving constant questioning is obviously a very active process as opposed to the passive reading of a fiction book for pleasure.

The *recall* phase follows the reading phase. We encourage recall to be done as recitation, since there is evidence that auditory memory is more lasting than visual memory (Tulving & Madigan, 1970). Recitation may be done by posing questions on recent passages and then answering them aloud with the book closed. When students hear as well as see the material, retention is increased because two sensory modalities have processed the information. Further, writing down the answers as well as reciting them associates even more cues with the information, specifically the kinesthetic cues associated with writing. In order to generalize the discriminative stimulus, recitation in different settings is encouraged so that recall does not become influenced by the specific visual cues of one location. Ideally, one could practice the recall and recitation phase in the room where testing will occur. The activity pairs the cues and stimuli of the room with the knowledge to be recalled.

Reviewing may be described as going over some portions of the previous phases, including some rereading and reciting of the most important materials. There is a danger of considering the review to be a skimming process covering all the material once more. It is better to cover selected material in depth and to concentrate on storing this material in memory, especially if the test will require essay answers. The first review is best done the day after the initial reading. Spitzer's (1939) retention study showed that the longer the first review was put off, the greater the retention loss (up to a 30% difference in recall). Thus, reviewing the day after reading and again right before the exam is preferable to reviewing twice right before the exam.

After the initial presentation of the SQ3R method, leaders model out loud their thought processes while using SQ3R to study various portions of a text. This modeling is important and may be followed by members imitating the leader, first out loud and then covertly.

The SQ3R method has been evaluated by Robinson (1961) and found to be very effective; however, there are some serious problems with the exclusive use of this model. Primarily, the model does not discuss important aspects of learning including storage of information. Assuming motivation, there still must be more to the process of learning than merely the surveying, questioning, reading, recalling, and reviewing of material. How is the material learned in order for it to be later recalled? This appears to be the primary deficit of the SQ3R method. Hopefully, this text fills in some of these significant gaps.

Note Taking

Exactly what are the most effective storage mechanisms? One important principle of storage is the organization of content. There is little, if any, disagreement among educators about the importance of organized note taking. The criteria for good notes may be said to include comprehensiveness and clarity; these are manifested mostly by the organization of the notes taken. It is almost as if the material must be nicely organized externally before it can be incorporated internally in an organized fashion. Neatness of the notes significantly affects recall as it helps the mind retain a visual image of the material. Lectures are sometimes presented in an unorganized manner leaving it up to the students to arrange their notes in some sort of comprehensible form. In such instances, taking down as much information as possible and organizing it while rewriting the notes after class may be the only effective process for organizing the material.

The leaders ask all members to share their current methods of note taking. The note-taking formats are presented with a stress on the importance of organization for memory storage. The efficacy of organization, specifically the use of hierarchical lists and sublists, has been empirically demonstrated (Bower, 1970). The organization of the material must be logical, meaningful, and visually clear. The actual physical structure of the notes must convey this organization. It is also important to underscore the necessity of being an active listener in class in the same manner that one actively reads. Members are given sample questions that can be used covertly in the classroom. These include the following:

How does one know this is true?
What are the implications of this, and how does it relate to other material?
In what context do I put this?

Finding the answers to these questions increases the student's involvement. Active listening and organization of material are important to any note taking.

The first format described is the usual outline form using Roman numerals. In the outline paragraphs are written as lists and sublists whenever possible. Each item has a cue word, and possibly a cue letter from each cue word; cue letters form a code word to serve as a mnemonic aid for the entire list. This cue word and letter strategy is encouraged for use with any note-taking formula.

The second format divides each piece of paper into three columns: the margin column and the remainder of the page divided in half. The far right-hand column is used for class notes; the middle column is used to outline readings, and the margin column is used for a few words to identify the topic.

Students usually want to spend some time talking about the importance of taking notes on their readings. Naturally, this importance varies from course to course. The student must discern how much to emphasize the readings as opposed to the lecture notes in each course. Readings related to topics discussed in class are of primary importance unless otherwise indicated.

Since many students underline in their readings rather than outline them all, some comments on underlining are relevant. Underlining more than 20 percent of the material usually makes the process meaningless. Using a system of colors reflecting priorities may seem to allow for more underlining; however, any gains must be weighed against time lost in picking up and putting down different pens over a period of hours. This cost benefit analysis leaves the system's value in question. Bracketing key lines at the side of the page is much faster than underlining and avoids visual obstruction of the material. Sometimes the underlining of information leads to an unconscious permission to forget it, as now the important knowledge has been disposed of in a tidy manner.

A process of integrating lecture and some reading notes throughout the semester may be used finally to boil down the semester's work into smaller and smaller outline packages. Students can utilize words paired with key concepts as well as headings with several cue words under each. The first letters from each cue word may be put together to form words. Several of these words may be put into a phrase or sentence and thus large amounts of information, if thoroughly understood, may be committed to memory as a package. In the process of learning lists, students must remember that there will be a clearer recall of those cue words at the beginning or end of a list, and a tendency to forget those words or cues listed in the middle. This phenomena is known as the serial position effect and is described by Benton J. Underwood (1966).

Underwood also describes another interesting concept that is profitable to share with study skills groups. This is the concept of massed versus distributive practice. Underwood's experiments lead to the conclusion that distributed practice (study), or practice carried out over a longer period of time, is more effective for long-term retention than practice done all at one time, even though the amount of study time is the same. Showing a graph of the results of distributive versus mass practice can be a very powerful tool. It can help convince students to distribute their study over the semester and shake the fantasy that they can learn a tremendous amount of material in a matter of days or hours. With discussion of this information and time for examples of the session should be complete.

SESSION VI

This session is begun by listening to group members describe the results of their experimentation with the SQ3R method of study and with note-taking. Their trials of different note-taking forms are passed around for observation and comments by group members. Typically, during this session the group leader must answer questions from group members about how to respond to the professor whose lecture seems totally disorganized. Deflecting this question back to other group members is often part of our response. We also reiterate previous descriptions of taking notes, especially the technique of forcing them into outline form sometime after class. In addition, we discuss how the student may disconcern what a professor considers important as well as the professor's philosophical biases; then we talk over how class information may be framed in that context.

A new topic for this session is that of the *meaningfulness* of the material. This is another of the critical factors left out of the SQ3R model previously described. Enhancing the meaningfulness of material is perhaps not only the most neglected area in study skills but also the most important. Retention is not merely a function of repetition since many things that are retained very well are repeated the least, as with Guthrie's (1959) "one trial" learning phenomenon. To some extent meaningfulness seems to function as an informal reinforcement system. The reward of a sense of satisfaction or mastery comes when new and previously unexplored material becomes known and integrated into material already understood. The connection between the formerly unknown and the known is itself reinforcing as it gives a sense of competency.

It is almost as if known material has an ability to draw as a magnet other related data to it. The forming of new associations with old information satisfies the motivators of curiosity, mastery, exploration, and the reduction of cognitive dissonance. These have been described by some as primary drives and therefore satisfying them is a form of primary reinforcement (MacMillan, 1969). The more meaningful the material is found to be by the learner, the more easily it is retained (Davis, 1935). Here *meaningfulness* is intended to denote some relation of the material to the student's needs or values.

In his work, Davis discovered that 75 percent of meaningful material was recalled after forty-five days, as compared to 32 percent of less meaningful material. Hopefully, nothing studied in school is totally meaningless or not at all related to the student's needs or values. Yet, it is clear that many students hastily conclude that much material is irrelevant to them.

Perhaps motivation to learn is increased when the material is perceived as meaningful due to what Clark Hull (1937) called the "factional antedating goal reaction." Put more simply, this would be anticipating the coming reinforcement or reward in the form of the material's utility.

Another aspect of the meaningfulness of material is its secondary reinforcement value. This comes in the form of grades, a degree, and hopefully a more satisfying life through the gaining of other types of reinforcement at a later date. This utilitarian approach to education is perhaps the case more often than not; insofar as we have focused on schedules, reinforcers, etc., our program also rests largely on secondary reward. Yet, in the meaningfulness of material there is something more.

In one group a nursing student was asked why she had remembered an esoteric bit of information concerning blood cells and not some other material of equal importance. If the anticipatory reinforcement hypothesis were to completely account for her learning, she should have reasoned forward in time that this knowledge would help her care for patients in the future; however, with further inquiry, she began to reason backward. The information was retained because it related to sickle cell anemia, a subject in which she held an interest. She explained that an interest in diseases particular to certain races had been a hobby of hers. This interest, in turn, had been spawned by an earlier concern with the theory of evolution and the development of species. In order to discover how far back this would go, the leader then asked how she had developed the interest in evolution. The answer was that in junior high school she had been a member of a conservative religious group that believed that the theory of evolution negated divine creation. She had joined this group because of her family's religious beliefs.

Through examining personal development of meaning in life, it becomes apparent that explaining meaning via regression is at least as convincing as doing so via anticipatory reinforcement. Further, if subsequent reinforcement were the only guide for learning, all useful information should have an equal probability of retention until reinforcement occurs.

The most helpful facts do not exist in isolation in the mind. Rather, thought constellations appear to exist so that a number of related ideas are clustered around a central idea that serves as the nucleus, the most fundamental or important concept in the cluster. This nucleus is also a cue that may be connected to any number of cues that serve as nuclei in additional thought constellations. This model of adjoining and ever-growing constellations of thoughts exists in the context of reinforcement theory, defined here as including the satisfaction of curiosity, mastery, and the reduction of cognitive dissonance as primary reinforcers. New material thus becomes meaningful when it relates to or hooks onto a familiar idea from another thought constellation; hence, the new idea and the subsequent connection or association is reinforcing as it confirms or relates to a previous idea. The mind may be likened to a funnel growing ever wider from birth to death with galaxies and solar systems of thought constellations inside.

These concepts are explained to the group in general manner, and a model is drawn on large poster paper in order to lend some concreteness to the discussion. The utility and beauty of this model for the purpose of study skills lies in its lending itself to visual understanding. Using this model, the goal of study becomes to relate as much material as possible to other familiar material by building connecting structures of ideas. X is to be remembered by associating it with Y, a previous known fact or concept. A chain of clusters of these meaningful associations should be built around a key nucleus of ideas that themselves are often anchored to other constellations by associational bridges or bonds. Group members are encouraged to form a visual image of some study material; perhaps they may even wish to picture entire chapters that have been converted to constellations by tagging cue words on each idea and labelling the associational bond or means by which they are connected.

It is recommended that a group spend one entire session on meaningfulness and how to stimulate meaningfulness as this appears to be a most significant factor in learning, and particularly in enhancing motivation.

SESSION VII

This session is begun by asking members to discuss which types of study material they find to be meaningful and which types they find not meaningful. They are encouraged to share any methods of making material more meaningful. Since this is such an important topic, the subject of making study meaningful may constitute the entire review in this session. It has been our experience that college students have more difficulty utilizing strategies about meaningfulness than other concepts thus far presented. This may be because college students generally have less experience from which to draw conceptual relationships than older people might. The students are asked how they have been able to relate specific material in their classes to former experiences in life or to other things they have learned through reading. In classes such as calculus and chemistry, the establishment of meaning may depend upon relating new material to other subject matter in similar courses. This basic material may be related to something even more concrete via a regression of meaningful associations going back to some fundamental concepts of calculus or chemistry try, concepts that may be concretized with images of real life experiences, analogies, or potential concrete events.

Making things more meaningful is a skill that must be learned and then practiced. Some students will be better at it than others, initially. It may be pointed out that learning this skill will require some mental energy, and the benefits of this investment will only be reaped over time. Greater benefits will be the result of extended and continued practice. Academic information once put in short-term memory must be incorporated into day-to-day conversation and thinking in order for material to be stored in long-term memory. This aspect of day-to-day utilization of material, at least to the extent of discussing it with others, is repeatedly stressed in the group as an essential tool.

The new topic to be introduced during this session is that of test taking. This section must be prefaced with a clear statement that no amount of test-taking skills can compensate for a lack of knowledge of the material itself. Nevertheless, some guidelines are important to recall during test taking if one is to use the test to demonstrate what he or she does know rather than what is not known. We also emphasize that organized and scheduled reviewing is a must. Test performance is greatly enhanced by some things that would appear to be obvious, but it may be seen, upon questioning, that many students have not even thought of these common-sense factors. Although many other students *are* aware of these factors, they may not use them regularly. A list of the factors relevant to test taking includes the following:

(1) analyzing the qualifiers on the test (i.e. *many, most, never, always*)
(2) carefully reading the instructions and the questions
(3) first examining the questions and then proportioning time during the test, noting which questions are worth more points, as well as which may require more time and which are more difficult
(4) carefully reading all of the options in a multiple choice question before choosing any one

It is particularly beneficial to examine the types of errors made on previous tests. Often bringing in sample examinations that have been corrected is helpful for this analysis.

Currently "test anxiety" is mentioned by many students as a problem. Deese and Deese (1979) feel that this is a defense the student puts up against taking the blame for his own lack of preparation. Often it may well be; however, all test anxiety does not appear to be motivated by secondary gain. Meichenbaum and Cameron (1974) have designed a "stress innoculation" treatment that may be used to treat test anxiety. Although it is similar to systematic desensitization, there is evidence that it is more effective (Meichenbaum & Cameron, 1973).

New findings (Kirkland & Hollandsworth, 1980, p. 431) indicate that a group treatment focusing on the acquisition of test-taking skills is superior in dealing with test anxiety to meditation and relaxation groups. It was found that

subjects in skills acquisition groups reported that they thought less frequently about their level of ability, less often about how much time was left, less frequently about how hard each item was, and less often about how poorly they were doing.

These subjects also reported improved concentration. While this may be a fair comparison between meditation and relaxation as opposed to a skills acquisition treatment, there was no actual stress innoculation group as described by Meichenbaum and Cameron contrasted to the skills acquistion group. This is a topic on which research is currently needed. Until this research is done and some findings produced, incorporating aspects of both approaches would appear wise.

Kirkland and Hollandsworth (1980, p. 431) identify the important aspects of test-taking skills as follow:

> surveying the length of the test, seeing if certain items or sections count more than others, assessing which sections and items will take more time, focusing on one item at a time, and marking more difficult items to return to later.

Other important test-taking skills not considered in the 1980 Kirkland and Hollandsworth article include the following: clues to the correct answer on grammatical grounds (e.g. agreement between the subject and predicate); marking a statement true only if there are absolutely no exceptions (e.g. if there has been one white crow anywhere at any time then all crows are not black); balancing options against each other (two options may be somewhat correct, but which is the more correct); considering all of the options; choosing the answer on the test in light of the instructor's philosophical biases or looking at the problem in the manner the examiner would, as many "correct" answers are matters of opinion; making sensible guesses rather than leaving an item blank if there is no penalty for incorrect answers; writing neatly in order not to offend the reader (exam answers with the same content may be graded differently without the professor being aware that he is responding to frustration over an attempt to read poor handwriting); and reading over the test before beginning as some questions themselves may be clues for the answers to other questions or may *be* part of the answer to another question on the test. Further elaboration on these points may be found in *How to Take Tests* (Millman & Pauk, 1969), which is a valuable reference source for students in a study skills program.

Self-quizzes are recommended to the group as being valuable aids in preparing for a test. During a self-quiz, the book should be closed, and answers should be written down for later evaluation by the student. It is common to fool oneself about how much has been retained from a reading; this activity provides a method of checking retention. Self-quizzes are especially helpful in preparing for essay tests. A prepared essay answer should have several points around a central theme, so that any point might serve as a cue for the entire cluster of responses. The notion of cognitive cues for the other cognitive responses appears valid and is supported by experimental data (Tulving & Madigan, 1970).

With group discussion of test-taking skills and a focus upon the aspects of those skills in which members believe they have deficits or strengths, this should be ample content for the session.

SESSION VIII

Session VIII opens with a discussion of the techniques that have been tried. As with the preceding session, this discussion may take up to half of the allotted time due to the large amount of material already presented. It is emphasized at this point that the ability of any tool, strategy, or technique to produce positive results depends upon how it interacts with the personality characteristics of the person using it. We continually encourage experimentation with different strategies until a set of those approaches that work best for that particular student has emerged. Consequently, the reviewing of strategies in the first part of each session may also emphasize trying something that a particular student has not tried before. This is simply an ideographic (individual) approach to study skills as opposed to a nomothetic approach (there is one right way to study for everyone, and the rest are wrong).

This new information presented in this session deals with different types of learning. This in no way pretends to summarize all the different definitions or modes of learning from an academic perspective. Rather it is an overview of some types of learning that we feel are most essential in making the most of an education and performing well academically.

Some school subjects, such as foreign languages, call for a large amount of *associative learning* or the learning of equivalents (i.e. A =).

When acquiring our native language we learned that *school* is the spoken representation of a building to which we go for instruction and learning. Now we must learn that *école* also means a building for learning. We may do our learning by pairing the words and learning that they are equivalents from two languages. We have learned another association to the object of the school building. If we think of this purely as "*school* is equal to *école*," then we are engaging in paired-associative learning. If we are linking each word with our mental picture of a school building, we are still doing associative learning, but with more items.

Associative learning is best done by repetition and rote memorizing; pairing it with images, if objects are involved, may be helpful. The criteria of learning is usually being able to produce the correct associations to the correct stimuli. Thus, when professor says, "1," the student who has learned successfully can reply, "A," and so forth. Most courses begin with some associative learning because it is necessary to comprehend the language of the discipline. In sociology the definition of "norm" must be learned (memorized). The understanding and ability to use the language precludes any higher operations or more difficult work.

In the social sciences and humanities, *conceptual learning* must take place along with the associative learning. Most disciplines require some conceptual learning; however, the social sciences must rely on it heavily as the phenomena with which they deal are often abstract. Conceptual learning requires delineation and differentiation, focusing on the boundaries of the term as well as the substance and properties of the object under consideration. For example, a student may be asked to list the properties and characteristics of a *crowd* and differentiate this from a *mob*. The student must be aware of the boundary between *crowd* and *mob*. To some extent properties of concepts may be observed, but often they must be inferred as expert opinion defines the properties of the concept and assigns it the term to be used.

A great part of academic performance is the ability to demonstrate the comprehension of concepts. Learning here may be defined as the ability to identify similarities and differences between and among concepts. This in turn requires listing and learning from rote as well as attempts that insight or at having a "working knowledge" of a process. The use of *working knowledge* here refers to the ability to take the object or concept apart and reassemble it, so to speak. If a student were to have a complete working knowledge of *city* as a concept in sociology, it would be important to know the attributes of a city, whether it differs from a *community* or a megalopolis, and if so, how. Moreover, the working knowledge of *city* might include its life cycle, developmental history, and how all of the parts interrelate to keep it an ongoing unit economically, politically, and socially. A working knowledge is the level of skill needed by a good mechanic not only to know the parts of an automobile engine by name but also to know how each part affects the other so that the engine might be taken apart and rebuilt. This degree of skill with concepts is one goal and one definition of learning.

Closely related to this is *problem solving* as a type of learning. If the names of the parts, their function and interrelationships, are known, then the student should be able to solve a conceptual problem just as a mechanic would fix an engine. Initially the student and the mechanic know the system is not in its proper state or functioning; consequently, this situation may be identified as a problem needing to be solved.

It is obvious that some standard exists for the car running well. Likewise, there is some definition (at least in the professor's mind) of how the problem is to be solved, although it may be less concrete and objective and although there may be more than one good solution. This is true whether the problem presented belongs to the realm of engineering; physics; psychology; sociology; history; philosophy; theology; the languages; or even literature, art, and music. All systems of knowledge have principles or rules by which goodness, health, correctness, or beauty are to be judged and known. As regards problem solving, helping a student gain skills that may be generalized is most beneficial, specifically in the process of moving from what is known to what needs to be known or from how things are to how we wish them to be. In mathematics, a certain unknown may be found by placing what is known in a specified, principle-given form; in a time/distance/speed problem, distance (miles traveled), if unknown, may be discovered by multiplying the time (number of hours) by the speed (miles per hour). Different juxtapositions and uses of the knowns by principles or rules and processes, in this case multiplication and division, will yield an unknown. Similar processes occur in problem solving throughout the natural sciences. The key requirements of these operations are as follow:

(1) The ability, if necessary, to translate terms from those given to the more general terms of a principle (e.g. recognizing that *miles* in this problem is the specific concrete unit of the abstraction *distance*, and that *miles per hour* is the unit of *speed*). It is more difficult to recognize these translations when solving complex problems than with the simple example given here. The student must also have the skills to allow for keeping all units of measure the same. Often minutes must be translated to hours, or units of measure converted to be on the same scale. The above problem might be represented rulewise as: m.p.h. X hours = # of miles, or speed X time = distance, or $X \times Y = Z$. The rules become more general with each representation.

(2) The ability to ignore irrelevant knowns and to focus on only the knowns necessary to find the unknown.

(3) The ability to recall the several possible principles that might be involved and to select, through the process of mental trial-and-error, which is appropriate principle. Eventually this becomes a faster process, more closely resembling recognition than selection. The speed with which this can be done is dependent to a great extent on the amount of practice given to it.

(4) Knowing from memorization and practice the correct steps of the process set forth by the principle.

These skills are relevant when approaching any subject matter concerned with solving problems. Different subjects will require different amounts of the types of learning identified here.

Along with the other types of learning mentioned here, *creativity* is also a skill to be learned. Being creative is necessary in order to perform at all in some courses; it will enhance performance in all courses when used judiciously with other skills.

We have discussed the working knowledge that enables one to take apart an object or idea and put it together again. Creativity may be viewed as the ability to put the object together again, but in a different way, so that something new and valued emerges. The qualification *valued* is important. Many can reassemble a process or product in a new way; however, that way may be seen as bizarre or useless rather than uniquely functional or beautiful. *Reassembling* here is used broadly, as in the reassembling of a series of musical notes, the reassembling of theoretical ideas to form new explanations for events, the reassembling of a kidney, or the reassembling of a process in which the kidney is involved.

Creativity comes to some persons with greater ease than to others. Although it might be argued whether one can learn to be more creative (Brogatta & Lambert, 1968), there is at least one improvable skill that is likely to lead to greater creativity. That skill is the ability to overcome *functional fixedness*, the habit of getting a certain *fix* or attachment to the usual function of an object or process. This *fixedness* inhibits the using of the object in novel ways. Novel procedures, even if conceived, may be omitted due to the discouragement often given for doing something in other than the most routine manner.

FOLLOW-UP SESSIONS

Session VIII is the last presentation of new material. One or more follow-up sessions are recommended to help students consolidate their newly learned study skills and assist them with any difficulties they encounter.

We advocate a follow-up session six weeks following the conclusion of the group, with a second follow-up session several weeks later. The purpose of these sessions is to review general principles discussed and to see how the students have been utilizing what they have learned in the group.

As a matter of course, some of the members of the initial group will not attend follow-up sessions. Likewise, there is very often a dropout rate during the first eight sessions resulting in a new loss of three people out of ten. We comment on this so that the leader will not feel that this dropout is necessarily due to personal style in leading the group. It is very possible that a student could obtain sufficient information to deal with his or her concern through attending only a few sessions. Inevitably other students, perhaps hoping for almost magical solutions, will decide that this program is not the answer to their needs; it may well be that the information presented thus far will not be helpful to these students because more pervasive problems exist. Many members of the group may be helped only partially by these cognitive behavioral methods, indicating the possibility that poor academic performance is simply a symptom of another problem. Poor academic performance may be related to the inability to express and experience feelings. It may be a means by which the student is self-destructive; it may also be a method of expressing anger toward those invested in the student doing well. In such cases, the fear of failure may be entangled with a wish for failure. Moreover, in the wish to succeed there may be fear of succeeding. Academic success may affect the student emotionally in ways that would not be obvious without further exploration of other aspects of the student's life.

Chapter 4

PSYCHODYNAMIC ISSUES

PROBLEMS not ameliorated by cognitive-behavioral methods are best approached on a one-to-one basis with a professional who has knowledge of psychodynamic principles and technique. The term *psychodynamic* refers to problem areas involving conflicting feelings that may be out of the student's awareness. Typically such feelings relate to the individual's strivings, wishes, and fears in a general way.

Some "psychological" problems that give rise to poor academic performance may be approached directly and resolved in as few as two sessions; others may never be worked through. If the student is not following through with strategies for improvement after gaining the necessary cognitive and behavioral skills, it is a consideration that a part of the student may be gaining some benefit from the present situation. The model presented here is analogous to Kaplan's (1974) *New Sex Therapy* as a treatment approach, but for a different symptom.

From a Gestalt point of view, it is most important that an alliance or working partnership be made with that "part" of the student that brings the problem forward. The treatment works toward eventual communication and access to that part of the student that is for some reason maintaining the problem. When the two parts achieve dialogue between themselves, as well as an understanding of each other, integration and resolution is possible. During this process resistance to change will emerge and need to be dealt with. A student may have varying degrees of awareness about his or her different "parts." The helper is now more in the role of therapist and must begin to assess the student's acceptance of the likelihood that these two parts of the self indeed exist. The degree to which the student is able to entertain this possibility indicates the degree to which there is reason to be optimistic about the outcome of treatment. At this point the helper may also glean some indication of the speed at which the student is able to move psychologically; thus an estimate could be made here of the length of treatment, including the ideal pace of observations or interpretations.

The student discussed here may be compared to a person who is overweight and professes only a wish to lose weight, yet indulges in overeating the day after beginning a new diet. Obviously one part of the person wishes to do one thing while another part wishes to do something else; each part is dominant at some time. Many explanations may be found for such behavior, and many benefits or psychological gains to an individual may exist. The causes of poor academic performance are as varied as are the causes of any other symptom.

A psychodynamic approach to treatment seeks to discover the meaning that lies behind a symptom. This meaning may or may not be conscious to the student. As with any treatment of this type, bringing the conflict into awareness will prove more helpful to some students than to others. The helper should gain an ample amount of data to support whatever formulation is reached, and hopefully the student will arrive at this formulation with minimal nudging from the helper.

Getting a complete and precisely detailed history of the problem will itself often reveal many of the necessary keys for understanding. The following questions may serve as a guide for the type of information to be gathered:

When did the student first recognize this as a problem?
If it has always been a problem, did it become worse at a certain point?
How does it happen that the student seeks help now?
What does the student want in specific, concrete terms?
What surrounding circumstances were present in the person's life at the time of the onset of the problem?
What significant events occurred just prior to the onset?
Were there significant happenings one year before the time onset?
What types of thoughts and feelings occur when studying is attempted?
When were there similar thoughts and feelings?
What, in behavioral terms, are the consequences of the problem?
What were the consequences at the time of onset, including reactions of others, and what were the student's responses to those consequences?
How has the student coped with the problem so far?
How does the student feel the problem developed and for what reasons?

There are a few typical motifs with the presenting symptom of study skills difficulties; however, there are frequent unique subtleties that may be overlooked if a therapist attempts to force the student into one of the typical motifs without due consideration for individual differences.

Perhaps the most typical pattern is the passive-aggressive posture whereby the student does little if anything to achieve in school and claims "no motivation" as the cause. It is often found that this student has extremely successful or demanding parents whose achievements cannot be approximated or whose expectations cannot be met; therefore, "Why try?" The student frequently hurts these parents indirectly by inflicting scholastic self-damage.

The parents may be relatively low in socioeconomic status and perceive the student as a possible redeemer. It is almost irrelevant whether or not the parents actually perceive the student as such. The key issue is whether the student believes they perceive him or her in this way. This pattern is likely to result in chronic anxiety, while the former pattern is likely to lead to a continued sense of apathy. Both may be equally debilitating during study.

This anxiety and apathy is most often the manifestation of a deep sense of frustration and anger that the student is keeping out of awareness. In this case, the benefit to the angry part of the self is the ability to express this resentment in a passive-aggressive manner while continuing to deny that such resentment exists. This permits a compartmentalized idealization of the parents to be protected with the part of the self that claims to wish only to do well for them. When the resentment emerges in therapy it must be accepted as is, with no interpretations or connections for a period of time, allowing the student to fully sense and feel anger. The student must also realize that this anger is being accepted, although not rewarded, by the therapist. Connections and interpretations are better received when the anger has fully ripened and is ready to blossom. A premature interpretation or suggestion of the role of anger in this case will frequently abort the entire process. Of course, it is best when the connection is not initially suggested by the helper. The focus in this case should be on the sense of burden the student feels from the parents' expectations. At some point in the treatment, the student will probably express anger toward the therapist, perhaps voicing dissatisfaction with the method, length, and results of treatment or even with expectations the student perceives as imposed by the therapist. This is the time to focus on perceived or real parental expectations. Alternative ways of expressing the student's anger, ways less destructive to the student himself, must then be found and used.

The following case descriptions should serve to better illustrate problems and therapy of a psychodynamic nature.

J. was the son of two physicians. His father operated a chain of clinics and earned over a third of a million dollars per year. J. came expressing a lack of motivation. He related that his father had been a poor immigrant who worked laboriously to go through college and medical school and subsequently became financially successful. The father was also described as impulsive, aggressive, and tyrannical; as a small child when J. refused to eat a particular food, the father poured it over his head. During early adolescence, J. had been berated continuously and chastised for not having accomplished enough in school. Even when J. had done exceptionally well, the father would frequently compare the son's progress to his own at that age.

Clearly J.'s sense of adequacy had been beaten down, as had all desire to achieve academically. Currently his best "achievement" was the lack of any achievement at all, which was the only way by which he could retaliate against his father and still claim to be in agreement with the father's goals for him. One of these goals was medical school.

In therapy J. was very passive, attempting through his passivity to reenact his relationship with his father. He did this by asking the therapist to tell him what to do and by carefully forgetting to implement any suggestions that were discussed, even though he had not been *told* to do anything.

It would be a critical mistake at this juncture for the therapist to be very directive, despite the fact that the student may be asking for such directions. What must occur is the processing and interpreting of what is occurring between the therapist and the student. The student should be helped to recognize the passive position being taken and that he or she is asking for things to be done, yet complaining if they are. In such situations homework assignments may represent orders from the father to the student. J. had always been punished for academic aggressiveness and effort by being told that it was not enough. Since he was punished for effort, initiative in pursuing academics eventually ceased.

In high school, J. had done well without any serious study. In college, J. found he had to study in order to maintain slightly above a *B* average, an average that left him eligible to do many things but that was just a hair beneath what would probably be required for admission to medical school. His subjective sense of the exacerbation of the problem did not become acute until late in his college career, at the "now-or-never" time for medical school.

During his treatment J. would frequently come very late or miss the appointment entirely; the therapist viewed this as confirming evidence of his use of passive-aggressive expressions of anger. When J. was led to formulate his conflict in terms of desiring his father's approval while at the same time wanting to express his fury at his father, he broke off treatment. This sudden breaking off shows a continued acting out of the pattern and refusal to give it up. This also highlights the importance of going slowly in treatment, of not being directive with those whose problems may involve reactions to overly directive parents, and of suggesting a possible interpretation when there is a relative certainty of it being accepted. It appeared that considering a more direct expression of anger was intolerable for J.; the benefits of being passive were greater than the benefits of accepting responsibility for his feelings.

S. came to a prestigious university on a scholarship. Upon arriving, she became intimidated by the social standing of many of the students she met and was partricularly impressed by their parents' income and social standing. Neither of her parents had graduated from high school and both made very low salaries. S. assumed somewhere in her mind that she must be a replication of her parents' inabilitiy, while her peers must be replications of their parents' ability. Thus she became extremely anxious about competing with these peers and felt doomed before she began.

S. had one brother, the "black sheep" of the family, who had done very little (other than get arrested) to call attention to the family and one older sister who was quite successful as a veterinarian. S. believed that her family's credibility rested on her; she would cast the deciding vote of whether the parents had succeeded or failed in the rearing of children. Consequently, she became extremely anxious about her performance. This anxiety in turn became debilitating.

In two sessions she was helped to see how she was assuming that she was a mirror image of her parents and that her peers were mirror images of their parents. The therapist confronted her about these notions and stated that these assumptions were possibly true, but not necessarily so. She was reassured that she had the ability to do as well as anyone else based on her test scores and performance in high school. Upon a two-month follow-up, she was found to be doing very well both in academics and in her social adjustment. A previous belief that she was physically less attractive than many of her peers, obviously not true, had been discarded.

It can again be seen in this case how important the history of the problem is as well as facts surrounding the current life situation, including self-defeating beliefs and their origins. Since academic performance often represents the winning of something other than just good grades, performance pressure in the academic world, as in the sexual realm, can inhibit performance itself. It is clear that the direction of therapy must be modified to fit the personality of the client. S.. unlike J., was not reacting to intrusive parents; she was able to utilize a more direct approach and see it as an indication of care on the part of the therapist.

R. came to therapy on the verge of failing out of school for the second time. The family history showed that her mother had never been satisfied with her husband, especially that he was an electrician. The mother had encouraged R. throughout his life to believe that he could do anything that he wished (in reality, anything that *she* wished). R. was pressured by his mother to attempt to be a physician, preferably a surgeon. She felt this to be the pinnacle of success. Unfortunately, R. interpreted this as a choice between being an M.D. (all good) versus a non-M.D. (all bad). Over the years R. had internalized his mother's views on this along with many of her beliefs and feelings. One of these feelings was that his father had been inadequate as a husband and that the mother deserved to have some adequate (perfect) male through whom she could gain deserved recognition (narcissistic gratification via association). Hence, the performance pressure that R. experienced was not uncontaminated; rather, it was quite tainted by his need to provide the mother with her adequate male. He also had feelings of anger toward his mother for expecting and demanding this. R. believed that to achieve the professional position of physician would put him beyond criticism and reproach (in short, make him "perfect") and that, if he did not become an M.D., he would simply be an inadequate person.

In this thinking R. projected the criticism that he feared his mother would give him onto society at large. He became extraordinarily self-conscious. Whenever R. would study any course related to his premedical curriculum, his anxiety would rise until concentration became impossible. He experienced overwhelming anxiety, debilitating confusion, and the inability to concentrate, none of which occurred when he studied any other subject. R. wanted desperately to win his mother's approval and love by giving her the man she had never had. Yet, while he was trying to become this ideal man, a part of his mind that was less accessible to conscious thinking was afraid of what the results might be, afraid that his success would, in essence, amount to winning his mother away from his father. R. loved his father very much and wished to be like him in many ways. This conflict was terrifying for R. While wishing to please and win his mother, another part of him was continually experiencing rage at her dominating, demanding character; further, if he were to win this battle and become a powerful surgeon, her ideal man, she certainly would not ever wish to let go of him. In essence, his battle resulted in an internal prison.

Needless to say, with this double approach-avoidance conflict R. was experiencing internally, the associated stimuli of the premed course textbooks heightened his anxiety. For R. the complexities of a conflicted life resulted in difficulty concentrating while studying certain material because the books were associated with the more pervasive but unrecognized conflict.

It did not take long in therapy for R. to see that his internal conflicts were disrupting his concentration when studying premedical courses. This was a powerful point in persuading R. to take some other subjects until his grade point average stabilized. With his obsessional mind, he was able to perform very well in philosophy classes. Eventually he majored in philosophy and maintained more than respectable grades.

The therapist continued to work with R. once a week for several months in order to clarify the many aspects of his problem. It was necessary to examine carefully what academic performance and studying meant to him at a deeper level. His desire to please his mother had to be placed alongside of his contempt toward her for being so demanding and controlling. The mother had placed R. in a situation in which he had to choose either her love and approval or his own sense of autonomy and self-acceptance. Further, R. very much envied and respected his father; R. perceived the father as being powerful, secure, and not particularly concerned with what others thought of him. While R. wished to emulate his father, he found himself struggling for the elusive approval of his mother who continually devalued the father.

Several delicate matters were involved in this case. R.'s wish for success and to please his mother was inextricably bound to his fear of success, as it would mean that he had submitted to her desires and suppressed his fury. Also, R. feared success because it would mean outstripping the idealized father professionally, which in turn, would deprive R. of his fantasy that the indomitable, powerful father could stand between R. and his mother's demands. Although the father had never actually done this, R. certainly believed that he could. The wish for success was bound to the fear of success and the fear of failure to the wish for failure, as each state would have its benefits and its price. Had R. fulfilled his mother's fantasies he, in essence, would have won her (a questionable prize) and each would have been bound to the other as the source of narcissistic supply. After a successful graduation, R. still dreamed of someday returning to take the premedical curriculum.

L., a woman in her late twenties, presented a similar difficulty concerning concentration while studying premedical material. At the time, she was a physician's associate with a P.A. degree and performed most of the functions of an M.D. Nevertheless, she wished to return to school for a four-year M.D. program in order to "fulfill" her "potential." She acknowledged hesitancies about pursuing the M.D. as she said it might, "rule out the family life which I desperately want." Yet, she recalled how her mother, having no career of her own, had been at her father's mercy. Her father had periodically indulged in extramarital excursions, and the mother, completely dependent financially, was left with little bargaining power. Thus, L. felt it was quite important to improve her competency and maintain autonomy.

While discussing her difficulty with concentration, L. recalled that in the eighth grade she had experienced a similar problem. She was asked about her life circumstances at that time and described that period of her life as marked by intense conflict between her parents. Often she would hear heated arguments that prompted fears in her that her parents would divorce and her father would abandon the family. Perhaps as a result of this period, L. worked for a stable and solid career. Her mother encouraged her, cautioning L. that she should avoid total dependence upon a man for financial support. Therefore, although L. grew up with the wish to find a man, she also had a parallel fear of being left by him or being forced to remain in a degrading situation over which she had no control. Consequently, the idea of marriage created an approach-avoidance conflict for L. She was, however, unaware of the source of this discomfort. She told the therapist that the most recent exacerbation of her concentration problem occurred at the same time a boyfriend moved out of town. This history lent support to the idea that L.'s difficulty in concentration was in some part due to an internal conflict that continued beneath her awareness; when she would study, her ambivalence about achieving the M.D. degree heightened because it was connected to her ambivalent feelings about marriage. Consequently, one part of her was working for the goal of good grades, while another part, fearing that no man would marry a female physician, was working against this goal. She experienced an internal feud whenever she attempted to study; the result was poor concentration.

L. was able to benefit from direct interpretation as she did not maintain a passive-aggressive posture and was capable of establishing a very solid working rapport quickly.

It is easy to see from the cases of L. and R. the importance of obtaining a complete history of the difficulty with study as well as the life circumstances surrounding onset and exacerbations. Information concerning the immediate precipitating events is also most relevant. As in the two previous cases, issues of sexual identity and identity, in general often manifest themselves in study problems. The historical data and other life circumstance data provide some demonstration to the student that there is evidence of another problem that is, at least in part, responsible for the resulting study skills condition.

In treating L. the previously mentioned conflicting strivings were pointed out, and she was ready to acknowledge them. In the second session, however, L. was unable to recall this primary issue of conflicted feelings and strivings, even though she remembered most of the other details of the first talk. She was at a loss why she had experienced no difficulty studying for the previous week and feared that if she did not continue with the therapist she would relapse. When she considered possible dependence on the therapist, she was quite concerned. The therapist then observed aloud that her interaction with him now appeared to be controlled by these same conflicting wishes (the wish to be gratified in a dependent manner and the wish to be autonomous). The initial observation regarding her wishes for and fears of marriage and medical school was repeated. Ths time the interpretation seemed to stay with her.

Although many more psychodynamic observations might have been made and continued treatment encouraged, there were no more short-term issue-focused interventions necessary to give L. an understanding of her impasse. Whatever path she chose in the future, she would have at least some appreciation of her ambivalence and how the two opposing parts of herself affected her in this dilemma. This is a success because the goal was not major personality change but rather to see the issues around one important area of her life. This understanding hopefully affords a person increased ability to tolerate and live with ambivalence regardless of choices made.

B., a second-year law student, came to the therapist for what he called "poor self-discipline" regarding drug use, alcohol consumption, and eating, as well as study habits. B.'s impulse control had been deficient as long as he could remember, but it became notably worse just prior to his entering college. He was the second of three sons born to an alcoholic father. His mother had worked as a waitress, struggling financially to keep the family together after the father had left. The mother then remarried to a man who physically abused the children until he too eventually left. At times B. had to steal in order to eat. He recalled his mother going out on dates and not returning until morning. B.'s older brother became heavily involved with drugs and "reckless" in most of his ways. Eventually this brother was killed in an automobile collision.

B. joined a wild crowd who used drugs and drank heavily. He always insisted on being the one who drove home, as he trusted himself much more than another to be in control.

B. was at first withholding in therapy. After several meetings, he was confronted on what appeared to be a lack of trust in the therapist. His previous comments about always wanting to be in the driver's seat were noted, and it was suggested that perhaps he was carrying this desire for control into therapy. He acknowledged this to be a trust and control issue; his mother and father had set few limits for him, and he now had problems with this due to poor modelling.

Although B. was able to feel anger toward his father, he continually denied feeling anger toward his mother. He would admit to "shielding" her. Eventually he came closer to sensing anger at the mother's inability to keep a man and the little care she gave her children. Much of the "self-discipline" problem was apathy due to a sense of numbness that B. had maintained in order to deny his aggressive and hostile feelings. When he let go of the numbness and felt anger, the sense of potency needed to tackle academics in an aggressive manner emerged. Nevertheless, B. still seemed to have an inexorable propensity for hurting himself academically.

At this point the therapist went back with B. to explore the circumstances of his brother's death. Just before B. had begun undergraduate school he had refused his brother's invitation to join him at a party. After the party his brother, intoxicated with alcohol and drugs, recklessly ran through a stop sign while driving home and was hit side-on and killed. Although B. had felt sadness at the time, he was in charge of funeral arrangements and had needed to remain "in control" of himself. Therefore B. had not fully grieved at the loss of the person closest to him. It seemed now that B. had taken on some of the reckless self-destructive aspects of his brother so that the brother's personality remained somewhat alive in B. The therapist realized that had B. accepted his brother's invitation to the party and gone with him, B. would have insisted on driving home as usual; consequently the accident might not have happened. Upon exploration it was found that B. believed this to be the case. After a period of experiencing suppressed grief, B. began to lose weight, attend class regularly, and appear more self-confident.

D., a twenty-four-year-old male graduate student in architecture, presented the complaint that he was spending enough time studying but was seemingly unable to finish large required projects. In assessing his current situation, he told of a daily pattern with literally no variety, including the tiresome repetition of a banana and a bologna sandwich for lunch and the daily wearing of a pair of jeans with a drab sweatshirt. He insisted that for recreation he wished to "accomplish something and be productive." Consequently, he would patch clothes, do laundry, or fix plumbing for recreation. D. went jogging; however, it was always at the same time and over the same course. He seemed to make all of his activities into work by the manner in which he approached them. He was completely concerned with the final product, giving little thought to the process involved in reaching this product. D.'s flat affect and the lack of luster in his eyes reflected the feelings of a man who simply could not enjoy himself, rest, or be at peace.

D. explained that he had always had, to some extent, a lack of "intensity" in his work, but that his motivation had dropped greatly this year. He attributed this to missing his usual summer vacation in order to finish his degree before a commitment to the Air Force began.

D.'s father had moved out of the home when D. was fifteen years old, and at that time D. began to keep continuously busy. He did chores at home and worked two part-time jobs, as well as going to school. He acknowledged that this keeping busy may have been, in part to defend against feelings of loss. Nevertheless, he maintained that it was hardly a loss as the father was never very active with him. D. perceived his father, who was also an architect, as being much more intelligent than he.

D.'s treatment began by an underscoring of the lack of variety and sensory stimulation in his life; it was pointed out that productivity would be enhanced by this stimulation as a means to motivate D. within his own value hierarchy. D. interjected that he would feel guilty if he allowed time for anything except his work. Rather than confront his resistance at this point, the therapist accepted this and asked where small changes for variety might be made while keeping D.'s time allotments the same. The first change agreed upon was to replace his daily banana with an apple or orange. Entire menus of different types of food were then considered, and it was proposed that D. wear some of the other clothes he already owned. Another change agreed to in the first session was to vary his place of study to two or three options beyond his office.

By the second session D. appeared a little happier. He reported a good week with satisfying accomplishments, as well as having enjoyed himself more. During this hour D. reflected on his relationship with his father and talked more of their home life, but without any greater depth. When questioned about his feelings of guilt when not constantly working, D. was very protective of his reasons.

Consequently, the therapist opted to pursue a cognitive-behavioral approach despite his belief that this was a psychodynamic problem. Treating a psychodynamic problem with cognitive-behavioral techniques may be effective in instances in which the therapist understands the dynamics of the problem and can intervene from that vantage point. There is a certain paradoxical aspect to this mode; it requires the therapist to enlist the client's cooperation by accepting the client's goal at one level (in D.'s case, "to be more productive"), and then to propose a new means of accomplishing this goal through which adjustment is made despite the goal. With D. the adjustment was to have pleasure by being productive in a greater variety of ways. Open termination after four sessions, he reported feeling better and being more productive.

In discussion of psychodynamic issues and study skills, it must be noted that many students use compulsive studying as a defense against social involvement and the forming of close relationships. Frequently, students who are studying more than enough and are doing well academically wish to join the study skills group. Such students often believe they should be studying even more. Initially they manifest what would appear only to be perfectionistic thinking. Upon closer examination of other aspects of these students' lives, it often becomes clear that compulsive studying is being used to avoid another important area of development. The treatment of this type of difficulty focuses largely on desensitizing the student to whatever is being avoided, along with some skills training for coping with anxiety-provoking situations. The avoidance may be examined historically. The assumption here is that the anxiety will decrease as the student becomes more comfortable with the anxiety-arousing stimuli and more skilled at dealing with those stimuli.

Chapter 5

FURTHER EXPERIMENTAL
UNDERPINNINGS AND
THEORETICAL ELABORATIONS

ALTHOUGH theoretical rationale and/or experimental support has been cited for most of the ideas and strategies presented in this text, the primary concern has been to present a service model. For these last few pages the experimental and theoretical aspects of the model are the main consideration.

In a chapter titled "Memory and Verbal Learning by" Endel Tulving and Stephen Madigan (1970) the significant aspects of learning theory from 350 BC to 1969 AD are reviewed. The primacy of association as the basis of learning is stressed. This includes associations of time and place. Hence, organization of material may be viewed as a type of association. Our model of learning emphasizes the necessity of forming associations between the new and the unfamiliar with that that is now known and understood as familiar. We have noted the benefit of seeing one thing as part of a large whole akin to the "redintegration" as defined by Tulving and Madigan (1970). The principle of redintegration asserts that a whole tends to suggest all of its parts once a part has been seen as a unit of the whole.

There is evidence supporting the use of mental imagery; subjects who were trained in and rehearsed imagery techniques performed at levels "stunning in comparison" to subjects utilizing rote learning (Tulving & Madigan, 1970, p. 457). Our advocacy of making words as concrete and pictorial as possible is based on this and similar conclusions by Arnold Lazarus (1976) regarding the utility and power of imagery.

The SQ3R method of study is grounded by the empirical confirmation of frequency theory, a component of the means by which information passes from short-term memory to long-term memory. The overt verbal rehearsal of information, as we describe it, is thought to prolong the residence of new material in the "buffer" between short-term memory and long-term memory, thus increasing the likelihood of more permanent storage (Tulving & Madigan, 1970).

Finally, a central thrust of our study skills model maintains that the meaningfulness of material is critical; for information to be learned it must be seen as meaningful in some way. In considering retrieval cues Tulving and Madigan (1970, p. 456) conclude that

> a necessary condition for the effectiveness of a retrieval cue seems to be the correspondence between it and some part of the auxiliary information stored with stimulus item.

In effect, this says that the cue must relate to the information in a meaningful way or that the cue must be understandable in the context of the other information. The understanding of one thing in the context of another makes the first item meaningful. Another sentence that alludes to meaningful reads: "Everyone agrees that appropriate organization facilitates recall" (p. 467). Is not *appropriate* organization in this instance synonymous with *meaningful* organization? Likewise, Glanzer (1972) finds that when semantically related words are close together in a word list the overall probability of recall increases.

We have argued that memory is aided by seeing clusters of ideas or constellations of data. Glanzer (1972) finds grouping effective, if not necessary, to shift information reverberating in the short-term memory of storage in the long-term memory. Along the same line of thinking, Gorden Bower (1970) emphasizes the importance of *hierarchical structures* or lists with sublists in learning. He concludes that this hierarchical approach proves superior as a strategy for retrieval in free recall. Hierarchical structures, groupings, clusters, and complexes may be seen as imposing meaning.

Although the methods of learning we have described utilize many cognitive-behavioral means, these methods rest on an epistemology or view of knowledge that is for the most part Piagetian (Furth, 1969). Piaget's perspective sees *knowing* as the activity of structuring the world. We have attempted to make explicit some methods of structuring and, therefore, methods of knowing the world. Furth (1969, p. 15) writes that, "To know is an activity." Our model advocates dialoguing with books and the constant interplay of questioning and answering in a covertly active manner. Knowing is always seen as an active dynamic relationship between the object and the knower; even the most elementary perceptual knowledge is the result of structuring by the learning knower (Furth, 1969). Thus there is little if any passive absorption of objective external reality. However, at this point we would like to allow for the possibility of some *latent learning*; this "learning" may be active at the unconscious level, with the associations being formed out of awareness and without intentional structuring or learning.

A distinction between remembering and knowing in the fullest sense is acknowledged in our model by contrasting the mere capacity to recall the parts of a whole as opposed to the ability to dismantle the whole and then reassemble the parts to form the original whole once again. Likewise Piaget's theory finds memory to be different from knowing; *memory* is more related to internal images or words whereas *knowing* concerns the actual conception of an image, the activity of constructing the world as we see it (Furth, 1969). This brings us back to the centrality of meaningfulness in the process of knowing and learning. To recall, remember, integrate, understand, or know, that which is to be known must be deemed meaningful by the learner for learning to occur. Furth's statements from the Piagetian perspective are congruent with this. He writes

> knowing is structuring . . . our structuring and constructing is identifiable with meaningful knowing behavior
>
> one cannot conceive of an organism unless it finds itself in some meaningful exchange with the environment (Furth, 1969,pp.15 and 244).

This leaves the student and the educator with the challenge of how to make material more meaningful and thus more easily learned. It might be argued at this juncture that the student should pursue only that which currently seems meaningful. While we encourage the student to study an area when it seems meaningful, we also maintain that other areas (including those which have been considered relevant only because they fulfill a curriculum requirement) may become meaningful. Whether they do become meaningful depends on the student's desire and ability to actively construct the material in such a way that it relates to other aspects of the student's experience.

The meaningfulness of objects and information is not formed

only out of what rewards or reinforcement there may be in the future for knowing them; meaning is also highly determined by the reinforcement immediately brought when objects or information are linked to other ideas or objects already known by the student.

If the source of meaningfulness is traced backward in time, it may be seen that a Pavlovian form of learning is at the vortex of the development of meaning. The stimuli to which the infant initially responds as though they are meaningful are those which have been repeatedly paired with pleasure and the cessation of frustration, usually via the satisfaction of some basic need. Consequently, many things about the infant's primary caretakers become meaningful and stay meaningful as long as the child is in a relatively dependent position. Therefore, just as a bell may become a meaningful signal for a dog if it has been consistently paired with food, many things associated with those persons who repeatedly bring physical and psychological satisfaction (or frustration) to the child become meaningful.

The young human discovers quickly those things which his parents or caretakers seek to have as well as those for which they show no regard. Subsequently, these adult caretakers and their values may be either imitated or rebelled against by the child. Indifference toward these perceived values or meaningful aspects of life will be extremely rare. We say *perceived* values as it is the child's perceptions, accompanied by all the possible distortions, that remain active in the child's mind; these perceptions may differ from what the primary caretakers say they find meaningful.

It appears that most of what a person comes to find meaningful and valuable is anchored in that individual's early experiences, particularly those experiences involving the primary caretakers. This is not to deny that countless other events and influences shape an individual's values and that all experiences, both internal and external, continue to transform these values. It is, however, to suggest that in order to make some new information meaningful and memorable, associating it with early, relevant, similar experiences or information is a powerful tool.

Motivational patterns and directions may also be found in significant early experiences. If a student is aware of these patterns and directions, including the strengths and the self-defeating aspects of motivational patterns, he or she is more likely to capitalize on their assets than be victimized by their weaknesses. With an awareness of the sources and pattern of motivation and an understanding of what is felt to be meaningful and more readily learned, the student is in position to become an active knower by utilizing various methods of structuring, organizing, and constructing the world.

This text has presented some of the methods we have found efficacious in helping students learn how to learn. The techniques are cognitive, behavioral, and psychodynamic in nature and have been selected for juxtaposition with a Piagetian view of knowledge. We have presented our mode of delivery utilizing paraprofessionals and the small group format with structured content for each session. The program has been very well received by students at the two major universities where it has been presented on a regular basis, as is evidenced by continued demand and positive student evaluations. The participating paraprofessionals have often expressed their pleasure with being able to help peers in a concrete way. The experience was a pivotal factor for some paraprofessionals who chose to pursue graduate study in a helping profession; others developed a marketable skill that proved valuable in their search for positions in university residence halls, dean's offices, academic advising offices, and counseling centers. Finally, the experience of training and supervising enthusiastic young paraprofessionals was personally rewarding for us.

BIBLIOGRAPHY

1. Anthony, W. A., and Wain, H. J.: Two methods of selecting prospective helpers. *Experimental Publication System, 9*:341-425, 1970.
2. Benedict, A. R., Apster, R., and Morrison, S.: Student views of counseling needs and counseling services. *Journal of College Student Personnel, 18*:110, 1977.
3. Bergin, A. E.: The evaluation of therapeutic outcomes. In Bergin, A. E., and Garfield, S. L. (Eds.): *Handbook of Psychotherapy and Behavior Change: An Empirical Analysis.* New York, Wiley, 1971.
4. Birdwell, J. A.: *Dimensions of Meaning in Relation to the Orienting Reaction.* University of Calgary, unpublished doctoral dissertation, 1972.
5. Blick, K., and Waite, C.: A survey of mnemonic techniques used by college students. *Psychol Rep, 29:*76-78, 1971.
6. Bower, G. H.: Organizational factors in memory. *Cognitive Psychology, 1:* 18-46, 1970.
7. Boyd, J. D.: *Counselor Supervision: Approaches, Preparation, Practices.* Muncie, Accelerated Development, 1978.
8. Brogatta, E. F., and Lambert, W. W. (Eds.): *Handbook of Personality Theory and Research.* Chicago, Rand McNally and Co., 1968.
9. Brown, W. F.: *Student Counselor's Handbook.* San Marcos, unpublished manuscript, 1967.
10. Carney, C. G., and Barak, A.: A survey of student needs and student personnel services. *Journal of College Student Personnel, 17*:280-284, 1976.
11. Carkhuff, R. R.: *Helping and Human Relations.* New York, Holt, Rinehart & Winston, Inc., 1969.
12. Danish, S. J., and Brock, G. W.: The current status of paraprofessional training. *Personnel and Guidance Journal, 53*:299-303, 1974.
13. Danish, S. J., and Hauer, A. L.: *Helping Skills: A Basic Training Program.* New York, McGraw-Hill, 1973.
14. Davis, R. A. *Psychology of Learning.* New York, McGraw-Hill, 1935.
15. Deese, E. K., and Deese, J.: *How to Study,* 3rd ed. New York, McGraw-Hill, 1979.
16. Dollard, J., and Miller, N.: *Personality and Psychotherapy.* New York, McGraw-Hill, 1950.
17. Furth, H. G.: *Piaget and Knowledge.* Englewood Cliffs, Prentice-Hall, 1969.
18. Glanzer, M.: Storage mechanisms in recall. In Bower, G. H. (Ed.): *The Psychology of Learning and Motivation: Advances in Research and Theory.* New York Academic Press, 1972, vol. V, pp. 129-193.
19. Guthrie, E. R.: Association by contiguity. In Koch, S. (Ed.): *Psychology: A Study of a Science,* Vol. II. New York, McGraw-Hill, 1959.

20. Hilgard, E., and Bower, G.: *Theories of Learning*, New York, Meredith, 1966.

21. Hull, C. L.: Mind, mechanism and adaptive behavior. *Psychol Rev, 44*:1-32, 1937.

22. Ivey, A. E.: *Microcounseling: and Innovations in Interviewing and Training.* Springfield, Charles C Thomas, Publisher 1971.

23. Jakubowski, P., and Lange, A.: *Responsible Assertive Behavior: Cognitive Behavioral Procedures for Trainers* Champaign, Research Press, 1976.

24. Kagan, N.: *Influencing Human Interaction.* East Lansing, Michigan State University, 1972.

25. Kaplan, H. S.: *The New Sex Therapy.* New York, Brunner/Mazel, 1974.

26. Kirkland, K., and Hollandsworth, J. G.: Effective test-taking skills acquisition versus anxiety reduction techniques. *J Consult Clin Psychol, 41*:431-440, 1980.

27. Kramer, H. L., Berger, F., and Miller, G.: Student concerns and services of assistance. *Journal of College Student Personnel, 15*:389-393, 1974.

28. Lazarus, A. A.: *Multimodal Behavior Therapy.* New York, Springer, 1976.

29. MacMillan, D. L.: *Behavior Modification in Education.* New York, McGraw-Hill, 1969.

30. Mahoney, M. J., and Thoreson, C. E.: *Self Control: Power to the Person.* Monterey, Brooks/Cole, 1974.

31. Meichenbaum, D., and Cameron, R.: *Stress Innoculation: A Skills Training Approach to Anxiety Management.* University of Waterloo, unpublished manuscript, 1973.

32. Meichenbaum, D., and Cameron, R.: The clinical potential of modifying what clients say to themselves. *Psychotherapy: Theory, Research and Practice, Summer*: 263-290, 1974.

33. Millman, J., and Pauk, W.: *How to Take Tests.* New York, McGraw-Hill, 1969.

34. Parloff, M. B., Waskaw, I. E., and Wolfe, B. E.: Research on therapist variables in relation to process and outcome. In Garfield, S. L., and Bergin, A. E. (Eds.): *Handbook of Psychotherapy and Behavior Change: An Empirical Analysis*, 2nd ed. New York, Wiley, 1978.

35. Robinson, F. P.: *Effective Study*, Rev. Ed. New York, Harper. 1961.

36. Rogers, C. R.: *Client Centered Therapy.* Cambridge, The Riverside Press, 1951.

37. Rose, R. G., and Carroll, J. F.: Free recall of mixed language lists. *Bulletin of Psychonomic Society, 3*:267-268, 1974.

38. Spitzer, H. F.: Studies in retention. *J Educ Psychol, 30*:641-657, 1939.

39. Truax, C. B., and Mitchell, K. M.: Research on certain therapist skills in relation to process and outcome. In Bergin, A. E., and Garfield, S. L. (Eds.): *Handbook of Psychotherapy and Behavior Change: An Empirical Analysis.* New York, Wiley, 1971.

40. Tulving, E., and Madigan, S.: Memory and verbal learning. *Annu Rev Psychol, 21*:437-484, 1970.

41. Underwood, B. J.: *Experimental Psychology*, 2nd ed. New York, Appleton-Century Crofts, 1966.

42. Zunker, V. G., and Brown, W. F.: Comparative effectiveness of student and professional counselors. *Personnel and Guidance Journal, 44*:738-747, 1966.

INDEX

71